"*No More Rotten Eggs*, the new bool[...] [...]at TG & Associates, is packed with useful [...] [...]d the right person for the right job, the firs[...]  [...]s with their new book contains dozens and [...] [...]cklists and other items designed to make [...] [...]eping grade AA employees easier than you ever imagined!"

John Stewart, President
QP Consulting, Inc., West Melbourne, Florida

"I found in Debra and Bill's book, *No More Rotten Eggs*, the kind of information that I wish I had had years ago when my managers and I tried to go about the hiring process. This book would have helped us avoid the many pitfalls in the hiring process."

Kim Patberg, Retired
IBM Corporation, Tucson, Arizona

"Thompson & Greif's *No More Rotten Eggs* is the perfect book for anyone who has to hire his or her own employees. Hiring the right person means having the right process to make sure you find the best candidate. This book provides a step-by-step process that shows you how to select one of your most important investments: your next employee."

John Giles III
The Giles Group, Winfield, West Virginia

"This book is both an inspiration and a manual for successful human resource development. *No More Rotten Eggs* guides you through the process of hiring and retaining qualified applicants. A must-read for political and organizational leaders, managers, and human resource departments."

Robin Fatovich, Internal Services Director
The Haven, Tucson, Arizona

"I am meeting with one candidate today and scheduling three more for next week. Your book has been a tremendous help!!! I LOVE the forms! I recommended your book to other business owners and told them it was worth the money just to have the forms."

Anne Oswald, Owner
Sir Speedy Printing, Olathe, Kansas

"This book is a great tool for leaders who are focused on selecting and retaining top talent. It is a comprehensive, step-by-step guide for getting hiring right. This is the foundation for gaining a competitive edge and building a successful and profitable business."

Merle Ballaigues, President
Thomas International Inc. (North America), Mississauga, ON, Canada

---

"Those of us in the printing industry have watched Deb and Bill become the leading authorities on human resources in our industry over the last several years. Now, they have applied the same principles to business in general and have produced a book that should set the standard for not only avoiding hiring rotten eggs but hiring golden eggs and growing them into real business assets. ***No More Rotten Eggs*** will be required reading for key staff at Allegra Network."

Carl Gerhardt, President & CEO
Allegra Network, LLC, Northville, Michigan

"Your success as a business owner is directly tied to how well you execute the hiring process. Debra Thompson and Bill Greif have created a hiring system that, when followed, will ensure that your new hires are Grade AA talent. At the end of the day, you'll sink or swim based on who you surround yourself with. Read their book and you'll be swimming all the way to the bank."

Steve Sanduski, CFP®, Managing Partner
PEAK Productions, Omaha, Nebraska
Author of Avalanche: The 9 Principles for Uncovering True Wealth

---

"I wanted to send you a quick note to tell you how much I loved your book!!! I found your book very easy to read with very useful information. Loved the CD with all the forms."

Kathy Morgan, Owner
Sir Speedy Printing, Irvine, California

"***No More Rotten Eggs*** provides a well-rounded approach to the hiring process starting with accurately defining the job and the skill sets of the individual needed. The book is chock-full of helpful tools that are also handily available on the CD-ROM that comes with the book, so you can quickly put the tools to use. ***No More Rotten Eggs*** saves the money and time it takes to unwittingly hire and then get rid of a poor performer. It's well worth the investment."

Suzanne Morgan, President
Print Buyers Online.com / Print Communications Professionals International (PCPI)
Arlington, Virginia

NO MORE ROTTEN EGGS

A Dozen Steps to  Grade AA
Talent Management

•

DEBRA THOMPSON
AND BILL GREIF

•

New York   Chicago   San Francisco   Lisbon   London   Madrid   Mexico City
Milan   New Delhi   San Juan   Seoul   Singapore   Sydney   Toronto

1 2 3 4 5 6 7 8 9 10 11 12 13 14 15 16   WFR/WFR   1 9 8 7 6 5 4 3 2 1 0

ISBN 978-0-07-166488-2 (book and disk set)
MHID   0-07-166488-2 (book and disk set)

ISBN 978-0-07-166490-5 (book for set)
MHID   0-07-166490-4 (book for set)

Interior design by the RBDI group, LLC / Aimé Carbone

McGraw-Hill books are available at special quantity discounts to use as premiums and sales promotions or for use in corporate training programs. To contact a representative, please e-mail us at bulksales@mcgraw-hill.com.

Inquiries should be addressed to:
TG & Associates, LLC
PO Box 32601
Tucson, AZ 85751-2601
info@tgassociates.com

CONTENTS

Contents of CD-ROM viii

Preface xi

Acknowledgments xiii

Introduction 1

The Hiring Process 9

    A Dozen Steps to Grade AA Talent Management 12

Step 1: Define the Job 19

Step 2: Define the Person 29

    Dr. Marston's Model of Behavior Chart 33

    Behavioral Characteristics Overview Chart 36

Step 3: Recruit 45

Step 4: Prescreen 61

Step 5: Employment Application 73

Step 6: Structured Interview 83

    Anti-Discrimination Guidelines 89

Step 7: Test 99

    Minimum Acceptable Scores

    Wonderlic Personnel Test-Revised 103

    Additional Thomas Profile Reports 106

Step 8: Reference Check 117

Step 9: Hiring Decision 125

    Sample Decision Matrix 127

Step 10: Make Offer 133

Step 11: Final Checks 141

Step 12: Eliminate the Rotten Eggs 151

Epilogue: Develop and Retain Your Grade AA Team 165

Bibliography 173

End-User License Agreement 176

Index 178

CONTENTS OF CD-ROM

The document names that follow correspond to the document names on the CD-ROM.

The Hiring Process
> A Dozen Steps to Grade AA Talent Management

Step 1: Define the Job
> Job Assessment Worksheet
> Customer Service Representative Job Description Sample

Step 2: Define the Person
> Human Job Analysis Form
> Classic Customer Service Representative Profiles

Step 3: Recruit
> Employee Referral Form
> Sample Customer Service Representative Internet Ad
> Classified Ad Placement Request Form
> Classified Ad Placement Log

Step 4: Prescreen
> Anti-Discrimination Guidelines
> Prescreening Questions—Customer Service Representative
> Sample Letter of Non-Selection (Resume)

Step 5: Employment Application
> Anti-Discrimination Guidelines
> Employment Application Form
> Driver Application Form

Step 6: Structured Interview
> Anti-Discrimination Guidelines
> Structured Interview Questions
> Top 20 Interview Questions
> Structured Interview Checklist
> Interview Response Form
> Candidate Evaluation Form
> Management Interview Questions
> Outside Sales Interview Questions
> Customer Service Interview Questions

Step 7: Test

    Sample Personality Profile Report

    Sample Emotional Intelligence Report

    Sample Wonderlic® Questions

    Wonderlic® Minimum Scores

    Additional Sample Profile Reports

    http://www.tgassociates.com/products/data/thomasPPAsamples.asp

Step 8: Reference Check

    Reference Checking Form

    Request for Verification of Employment Form

Step 9: Hiring Decision

    Decision Matrix Form

    Decision Matrix Sample

Step 10: Make Offer

    Sample Offer Letter

Step 11: Final Checks

    Background Check Release Form

    Sample Letter of Non-Selection (Interview)

Step 12: Eliminate the Rotten Eggs

    Termination Planning Checklist

    Termination Checklist

Additional Resources

    http://www.tgassociates.com/asp/hrLinks.asp

Popular Internet Job Boards

    www.careerbuilder.com

    www.craigslist.org

    www.dice.com

    www.hotjobs.yahoo.com

    www.job.com

    www.jobing.com

    www.monster.com

    www.regionalhelpwanted.com

    www.snagajob.com

    www.theladders.com

    www.tgassociates.com

PREFACE

Business success depends on the presence of an effective labor force: employees who are competent, stable and well-led. That can only happen when managers are truly diligent in finding, developing and retaining top performers. But that is very difficult for most business owners and managers. Our focus over the years has been providing the tools and products that overcome this difficulty.

In 2000, we wrote and published the How To series—*How to Hire the Right Person the First Time, How to Develop Top Performers*, and *How to Retain Top Performers*. Since then, we have been practicing what we preach. We employed the tools that we defined in those books to help companies raise the bar on their people management processes. In particular, we have used our hiring process to conduct customized recruiting for companies across North America.

Not only did our experience validate our process, but it helped us develop enhancements in all phases of that process. It also pointed out that the original How To series needed an upgrade to incorporate these enhancements. We actually started the update in 2006. We always had intentions to refresh all of the books of the How To series, but the changes in technology were happening so fast, we decided to focus on the hiring process first.

The feedback from business owners and managers clearly pointed out that most companies' hiring processes were broken. Companies were investing heavily in recruiting efforts that, at best, produced only warm bodies. We felt it was essential that our new book emphasized the need to do something different, and that is why we titled it *No More Rotten Eggs: A Dozen Steps to Grade AA Talent Management*. The title defined the need for not only acquiring only Grade AA talent, but eliminating the rotten eggs so you have a Grade AA team.

This book is the first of its kind to fully document the entire hiring process and recommend the specific tools needed to be successful. There are many books related to hiring, but most focus on specific aspects rather than the whole process. This book also addresses one of the most dreaded tasks—elimination of the rotten eggs.

Now that we have finally launched *No More Rotten Eggs*, we sincerely hope you find this the most valuable resource you have ever seen for hiring success.

ACKNOWLEDGMENTS

Completing this book has been a major part of our lives for the past several years. To grow our business, we knew we had to publish a book that conveyed our beliefs and our passions about the processes that have helped companies—including our own—grow with a competent, stable, well-led team. The writing process has been more difficult than we projected, but with the help and support of many people, we were motivated to make it happen.

First of all, we want to thank all of our clients who over the years have helped us validate our hiring process. They are the people who told us that it worked and who encouraged us to "spread the word."

We also want to thank Dina Lacandola, who helped us by "walking the talk" every day in assisting clients with their unique hiring needs. Her contagious enthusiasm contributed to every facet of creating the processes and marketing the book, our products and our website. She also, like us, has read the book over and over to help us with its clarity and accuracy.

We sincerely appreciate the efforts and the support of Merle Ballaigues and Scott Mackintosh at Thomas International who helped us present the profiling process and supported our efforts from the beginning.

We also appreciate the input from Reuven Bar-On who reviewed the section on emotional intelligence and provided input to clarify this important part of Step 7.

We would have been lost without the help of Aimée Carbone at The RBDI Group who worked extremely hard to design the cover and the look of *No More Rotten Eggs*. Her energy and enthusiasm made it easier for us to keep at it and get the original book finished.

Our fond thanks to Ken Chaletzky and Laura D'All at Copy General who worked with us from the beginning to help us visualize ***No More Rotten Eggs*** as a finished product. They also gave us valuable feedback and recommendations that were much appreciated.

Finally, we thank you, the reader, for buying this book and supporting our efforts to build competent, stable, well-led teams within any size business, organization or department.

Debra Thompson
Bill Greif

INTRODUCTION

Hiring the right person, like buying eggs, is not an easy undertaking. When we go to the market to buy eggs, do we just grab a carton off the shelf and put it into the shopping cart? Of course we don't. We open the carton to make sure all of the eggs are intact and fresh. We don't want cracked or spoiled eggs. We may go through several cartons before we find the one we like with fresh, unspoiled, uncracked eggs. Why don't we use as much care in our hiring process? The evidence points out that, instead of getting the top performer we set out to find for our business, we often end up with a "rotten egg" who scrambles our efforts to build a top-notch team. According to management guru Peter Drucker, "One third or more of all hiring decisions are outright failures and in no other area of our business would we tolerate such dismal performance."

It is another truism in recruiting that "We hire for skills and fire for behaviors." Studies show that 46% of all new hires fail within 18 months, not because they didn't have the skills, but because they did not "fit" the team. Only 11% fail for lack of technical skills.

Consider also the following statistics from the Department of Labor, the Department of Commerce, and the National Institute of Occupational Safety and Health:

- 30% of all business failures result from poor hiring techniques
- 33% of all employment applications are falsified
- 45% of all resumes contain false or exaggerated information about job experience, education, etc.
- One out of 20 applicants falsifies a name, Social Security number, or driver's license number
- Embezzlement is a $6 billion industry

These statistics are not exaggerated; in fact, they may be understated. But they are alarming and should catch your attention. The old "hit or miss" method of staffing, which lacked depth and discipline, may bring you a "warm body," but it will not attract the quality talent you need.

The examples of bad hires—"the rotten eggs of the organization"— go on and on. It is clear that we need a new paradigm to eliminate the rotten eggs. More importantly, we need tools to find Grade AA talent. No longer are we just looking for A and B players, but for a whole new measure of quality—Grade AA.

In his book *The Human Equation: Building Profits by Putting People First*, Dr. Jeffrey Pfeffer said, *"All that separates you from your competitors are the skills, knowledge, commitment, and abilities of the people who work for you. . . . Companies that manage people right will outperform companies that don't by 30 to 40 percent."*

McKinsey & Company in its study "War for Talent" clearly identified the value of top performers with these results:

- High performers in operations will increase productivity by 40%
- High performers in management will increase profits by 49%
- High performers in sales will increase revenues by 67%

Aren't those the results that you want in your business?

In its 2006 study the Corporate Leadership Council revealed that employee engagement has a "significant impact on both employees' levels of discretionary effort and their intent to leave an organization. Increased engagement may contribute a 57% increase in discretionary effort and as much as an 87% reduction in the desire to leave a company."

Today, thriving companies are raising the bar on their human assets. Jim Collins, author of **Good to Great**, said, *"The old adage, people are your most important asset is wrong. People are not your most important asset. The RIGHT people are."*

Flourishing companies have realized that they get the best return on their investment by creating a competent, stable, well-led workforce. They have systems and processes in place that enable them to hire the right people the first time. These successful companies continually raise the bar and upgrade their leadership so their staff will continue to be well-led. In addition, they create and promote a culture that ensures they will retain those top performers.

Ian Marshall, senior manager of employment, Southwest Airlines, in an article in *Go Jobing Magazine*, said it best. "Investing time and money on recruiting the right people pays off—after all, the people are what separates ordinary businesses from extraordinary companies. When it comes to ROI, it costs more to hire the wrong person than it does to be selective. That's why we won't just hire someone to quickly fill a need."

One of the greatest challenges you will have to face in raising the bar will be your ability to attract top performers. Finding qualified people has always been a challenge. Leading up to the economic downturn in 2008 and 2009, the futurists predicted that we would soon be in the midst of a serious labor crisis. The experts estimated that the United States would face a shortage of roughly 10 to 14 million qualified employees by 2020 (depending on who you listen to). That was based on the view that the baby boomers would be retiring and there would be fewer people in the succeeding generations to replace them. As unemployment in 2009 approached 10%, there was an expectation that hiring for those companies wanting to add staff would be easy. In truth, hiring continued to be difficult as the available applicants lacked the skills and the aptitude to handle the highly technical jobs that needed to be filled.

There are other complications in the search for that top performer. You are not only competing for the best skills and experience within your own industry, you will be competing with other industries as well. Many of the skill sets and talents needed today are transferable across many different industries. As the battle for talent intensifies, employee recruitment and selection has never been more critical. For these and a myriad of other reasons, the dynamics of staffing has changed. You will need to revolutionize your staffing practices if you plan to be a successful business. Just as in every other aspect of your business, you must put a process in place that will guarantee success in all of your staffing endeavors.

CEOs and managers spend many hours developing business and marketing plans and evaluating facility and equipment purchases. Yet they leave the planning for the human side of business to the end, so when the need arises for adding staff, there rarely is a plan and process in place. The result is a staffing effort that focuses on the "warm body" approach that delivers another "rotten egg." The consequences of a bad hire can destroy a business. Consider the wasted investment completing the hire, the wasted hours of training, the loss in productivity due to poor performance and the poor morale that permeates the entire company because of attitude issues. Needless to say, ultimately you'll experience a loss of customer confidence and lost sales. The cumulative effect can be disastrous.

The human side of business requires attention to organizational planning and the development of staffing strategies. It dictates nurturing a culture that recognizes the value of people in achieving the company vision. It requires "hardwiring" that culture so the entire team is tuned in and aligned with it. *Good companies don't just happen.* Visionary leaders know what it takes to build a strong team and they take the actions to make it happen.

Hiring is no longer a simple matter of filling job openings. To be successful, you and your hiring managers are wise to use a multi-dimensional process. This process must be validated and have as its projected output Grade AA quality hires the first time and every time. This book explains how to set up and implement such a process.

We have designed this book to help you find your Grade AA talent. It clearly explains the process and provides the tools and information you need to implement it and develop your staffing skills. This process uses a formula that has been proven to be extremely successful. Follow it step by step, apply its principles, use the recommended tools and you will find success at the bottom line.

Whenever we mention a form or document that you can find on the accompanying CD-ROM, you will see this icon. See page 176 for the terms and conditions governing your use of the CD-ROM before you open the seal on the CD-ROM envelope.

Please note that you will find many more forms on the CD-ROM than those specifically referred to in the book. All of the information is identified on the Contents of the CD-ROM page and in the interactive listing on the CD-ROM itself. The CD-ROM also provides access to the TG & Associates website's interactive listing of additional human resource information. This listing is regularly updated.

THE HIRING
PROCESS

THE HIRING PROCESS

*Based on years of research and experience, we have created
a process that clearly defines and explains the steps to hire
the right person the first time—every time.*

Successful businesses develop and follow processes designed for success in everything they do. Consider the emphasis on Kaizen, Six Sigma and ISO 9000. Setting up and following a disciplined process for hiring must be no different. Adopting the techniques described in this book ensures the best possible fit for the job and your business. Through the customized recruiting services provided by our company, TG & Associates, we have validated this exact process by assisting companies throughout the U.S. and Canada in finding and hiring Grade AA talent. It has proven to be extremely successful for them, and we guarantee it will be successful for you, too.

When we first started doing business consulting, we defined *Thompson's Ten Principles for Success*, a process flow that moves from a plan to profit in a logical, visible sequence. Business success depends on following and accomplishing all ten principles. *No More Rotten Eggs: A Dozen Steps to Grade AA Talent Management* is no different. It too starts with creating a plan and ends with successfully filling a position with a top performer. Your goal is not only to avoid the "rotten eggs" but to find Grade AA talent and develop each find into the "golden egg" that will make your business successful. A full carton of "golden eggs" will be the culmination of your efforts. You will have Grade AA talent, truly engaged and performing, and working together to gain the competitive advantage that will make your business succeed. The steps of this process are logical and sequential, and each is essential to meeting your goal.

An article in *Go Jobing Magazine* stated, "Don't let open positions stagnate while hiring managers churn through reams of resumes from unqualified candidates. Put a process in place based on a technology framework. It is imperative that productivity efficiencies become an integral part of your talent management strategy in order to reach and review more candidates faster."

At certain points in the process, you will reach decision points. These are intended to make you evaluate your progress and decide whether you should proceed with a particular applicant. Staffing is time consuming, so you do not want to continue through the entire process with all applicants when it is obvious they will not be a good fit.

It is important to recognize that hiring is a difficult and daunting task for anyone. Therefore, it is vital that the person doing the hiring follow the process step by step and do it right or pay costly consequences. Often, the discipline to follow the process overwhelms hiring managers and they take shortcuts and skip steps. When they do, invariably the business will experience the costs of a poor or bad hire.

In addition, with the growing shortage of "qualified" people in the labor pool, finding the right person takes longer than it used to. If the quality of the available candidates may not be right at the time you begin your search, the situation demands more discipline and patience from staffing managers to stick with the process. They will need to continue to be diligent in their search until all of the requirements are met.

Each step in the hiring process is so critical, in fact, we have devoted a chapter to each of them. It not only gives you an understanding of the details but also provides ideas, suggestions, forms and tools to successfully complete each step. To help keep you on track, we have provided a visual guide to **A Dozen Steps to Grade AA Talent Management** and included a brief summary of the purpose of each step. The subsequent chapters detail all the steps and show how to accomplish each one and measure whether you are ready to move on. As you read our book, it may become obvious that to raise the bar within your company, you will have to let some people go.

Our goal is to give everyone involved in any part of the hiring process the tools needed to make a successful hire the first time—every time. All of the companion tools and resources mentioned in this book are included on the accompanying CD-ROM.

WARNING:
DO NOT shortcut the process!

It will be hazardous to your business!

A DOZEN STEPS TO GRADE AA TALENT MANAGEMENT

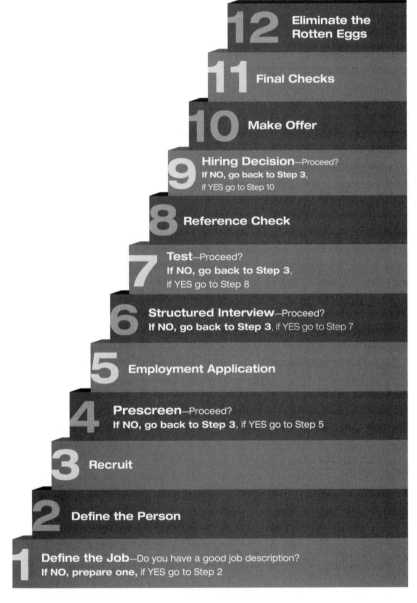

12 Eliminate the Rotten Eggs

11 Final Checks

10 Make Offer

9 Hiring Decision—Proceed? If NO, go back to Step 3, if YES go to Step 10

8 Reference Check

7 Test—Proceed? If NO, go back to Step 3, if YES go to Step 8

6 Structured Interview—Proceed? If NO, go back to Step 3, if YES go to Step 7

5 Employment Application

4 Prescreen—Proceed? If NO, go back to Step 3, if YES go to Step 5

3 Recruit

2 Define the Person

1 Define the Job—Do you have a good job description? If NO, prepare one, if YES go to Step 2

A DOZEN STEPS TO GRADE AA TALENT MANAGEMENT

STEP 1: DEFINE THE JOB

The nature of the position to be filled is defined and the expectations are determined. The existing job description is evaluated against the job function to see if it is accurate. If it is not, then make the necessary changes. If a job description does not exist, prepare one so that all applicants and the staffing manager can agree on the responsibilities and duties of the job.

STEP 2: DEFINE THE PERSON

Use the Human Job Analysis (HJA) to identify the specific behavioral expectations required for the position, your business strategy and your organizational culture.

STEP 3: RECRUIT

It is critical to get information about your staffing needs out to the right audience. The recruiting campaign must be designed and executed to attract the individuals most likely to meet your requirements.

STEP 4: PRESCREEN

You will have several opportunities to quickly weed out applicants who are clearly not viable candidates. Verifying minimum requirements and checking for red flags is essential at this step.

STEP 5: EMPLOYMENT APPLICATION

This legal document gives you the information you need to understand the applicant's background and skill experience. Use of an approved state and federal compliant application form is critical. The application should include a release to conduct reference checks.

STEP 6: STRUCTURED INTERVIEW

Prepare for this event. Know the right questions to ask and do not hesitate to use a script to keep on track. Record the responses you get for use in the decision process.

STEP 7: TEST

Tests are recommended to measure math aptitude, comprehension, and on-the-job skills. Additional assessments to determine such things as personality fit, emotional intelligence, sales abilities and other characteristics are given at this juncture of the process.

STEP 8: REFERENCE CHECK

You cannot assume all the information you gather in the resume, application and interview is accurate. Reference checks will enable you to verify the data and gain additional insight into previous employment behaviors of the applicants.

STEP 9: HIRING DECISION

Objectively evaluate all of the qualified applicants against the hiring criteria. Create a matrix to rank-order each candidate to select the best.

STEP 10: MAKE OFFER

You may make a verbal offer, but immediately follow it with a full written offer including all details of the offer and any added requirements such as I-9 verification, drug and medical tests.

STEP 11: FINAL CHECKS

A background investigation is prudent and necessary for liability protection. It is an essential step in the final selection of the best employees. If your policies require it, also have medical and drug testing performed by competent agencies.

STEP 12: ELIMINATE THE ROTTEN EGGS

The first 11 steps of this book dealt with the problem of helping owners and managers add new staff and ensuring that each new hire possessed the skills, aptitudes, intelligence and personality to occupy those critical seats on the bus. Now in Step 12, we complete the full dozen steps by ensuring the rotten eggs are eliminated from the ride. It is absolutely essential that the unwelcome and unproductive employee is dealt with.

"No matter the size of your company, a better talent plan than your competitor's that is successfully executed and measured will result in increased profits."

Rusty Rueff and Hank Stringer, Co-Authors of
Talent Force: A New Manifesto for the Human Side of Business,
Prentice-Hall, 2006

STEP 1
DEFINE THE
JOB

STEP 1: DEFINE THE JOB

*To successfully function within a business,
all employees need to understand their duties and
responsibilities and know how they interface with
every other employee and with management.*

The longest journey begins with a single step. The journey to hire and develop a "golden egg" is the same. Before any hiring can be accomplished, it is necessary to have a clear picture of the position that must be filled. All too often, ads are placed and interviews are initiated before the staffing manager has accurately articulated the requirements of the position. The job requirements involve more than a mere statement of duties. They also require defining the vertical and lateral relationships for that position and every other position within the organization. These relationships must be further defined in terms of the functions to be performed for the business to create its products or deliver its services. When correctly performed, these functions result in the successful execution of all of the processes involved in delivering the product or service as well as managing and evaluating the capabilities of the business.

We strongly believe that organizational success depends on a clear understanding and implementation of the internal customer concept. That is, every individual in a particular process is the customer of every other individual in the process. Designing the infrastructure and the processes makes clear to each of the individuals who their internal customers are and what the expectations are for what must be delivered to that internal customer. Having clear functional responsibilities and defining internal relationships guarantees that the final product or service will be of high quality and meet the expectations of the external, paying customer.

Evaluate the Infrastructure

We recommend that you review and update the infrastructure as part of an annual process. In addition, if you need to bring on additional staff during the year, it is essential that organizational relationships be reexamined to define how the functions of this new hire will fit into the infrastructure.

As Jim Collins addresses in his book, *Good to Great*, "You must have the right seats on the bus, the right people in the right seats and the wrong people off the bus."

No matter how big or small your company is, you must define its functions and relationships in terms of an organization chart. Defining hierarchy helps departments and individuals visualize their roles in meeting the overall company vision. Each of the positions must contribute to the accomplishment of the mission of the organization and the achievement of the vision. Once these functional positions are established, then and only then can the right person be selected to fit that function.

While the emphasis might be on finding a new employee, it is essential that job functions for existing employees are correctly defined. Particularly when company growth and sharing functional activities has prompted new hiring, then the new and existing job functions must be compared to ensure that any division of responsibility is clearly defined.

Too often people are put into a positions where they are not able to fulfill all the requirements of that function. This can mark the beginning of numerous breakdowns within the organization. The success of a business depends on working within the functions rather than working around people. When people are put in positions without the right qualifications, they cannot fully perform the intended function, which gets compromised. Then other people have to step in or be assigned to pick up the pieces. For these reasons, it is critical to capture all the requirements of the position, and be able to articulate them in such a manner that personnel can be evaluated, trained and measured against the criteria.

The necessary information required for a job function is captured through a Job Assessment Worksheet. The job assessment is a disciplined approach to gathering and organizing the necessary information in the job description prior to beginning the recruiting and selection process.

Without a clear understanding of the job, neither the staffing manager nor the applicant can be sure that needs are matched.

Determination of the job requirements should involve all personnel who have a stake in the position. This clearly includes the CEO and the managers, but it could include peers who will interface with the job and other department managers who depend on the output of this position. Descriptions are most accurately formulated when supervision and the employees who have a working knowledge of the mechanics of the job provide combined input. Involve your existing employees in the creation of the job assessment. In particular, if, like many companies, yours does not have job descriptions for every employee, take action now to put them in place.

On the accompanying CD-ROM, you will find the Job Assessment Worksheet. Print it out and use it to gather essential information for the new job position or to reexamine the existing position.

Today's Date:

Position Title:

Reports To:

Defined By:

Do you have a written job description? Yes ❑ No ❑

IF YES, re-evaluate the job description after completing this Job Assessment Worksheet to capture any changes or to verify that all information is current and accurate. IF NO, complete this form and use it as basis for creating a current and accurate job description.

Company Name: _____ Position Defined by: _____ Date: _____

Position Title: _____ Ideal Start Date: _____

Department: _____ # of Employees in this Department: _____

# of Employees in the Entire Organization: _____

Purpose: Temporary Regular Full Time Regular Part Time Casual

FLSA Status: (Check one): Non-Exempt ❑ Exempt ❑
(Check one): Salary ❑ Hourly ❑ Commission ❑

Pay Range: (internal use only) Salary: _____ or Hourly _____ to _____

What are the incentives or bonus plans in place for this position? If so, please explain: _____

Interview Team: _____

Job Summary (Briefly describe what the position was created to accomplish).

Is this position opening to be kept confidential? Yes ❑ No ❑

Is this position: New ❑ Replacement ❑

If replacement, name of employee being replaced: _____

Reason for replacement: _____

If there is something the last person who held this position did that you want the next person to do, please explain: _____

If there is something the last person who held this position did NOT do that you want the next person to do, please explain: _____

Total number of people hired for this position during the past year? _____

If supervisory position, how many employees will they be supervising? _____

page 2

...ny benefits, rules, regulations and policies? Yes ❑ No ❑

...n a separate sheet, list in order of importance the essential functions of the job and ...: describe what must be accomplished, not how it must be done; include supervision ...ysical, mental and perceptual functions of the job.)

...rategize, conceptualize and plan?) Yes ❑ No ❑

Overview of a Job Description

TA well-written job description is one of the most valuable tools you will have when it comes to hiring and managing people. Job descriptions show how the goals of the company are translated into individual duties and responsibilities, while being an excellent tool for communication. A well-prepared job description is a must-have for recruiting, interviewing, orientation, training, coaching, disciplining and overall managing.

If you do not have a complete, current and accurate job description for the position you are hiring for—

DO NOT proceed to Step 2
until you take the information from the
Job Assessment Worksheet and create an accurate
job description for the position.

WARNING: If you choose to continue the hiring process without an accurate job description for the position, you have already increased your chances of a bad hire. Remember, the reason for following this process and completing each step is to ensure attracting Grade AA talent the first time and every time.

Do not rely on existing job descriptions. Once you have assessed the job and completed the Job Assessment Worksheet, compare it to the existing job description—if you have one. Continually reassess each position as your company moves forward. The job description should focus on the job requirements based on the completed Job Assessment Worksheet. Purchasing new equipment, updating technology, implementing a new process or hiring a new employee warrant the need to reevaluate the functions and update the job description.

Elements in a job description must represent bona fide occupational requirements. They cannot discriminate against any protected group and must be in writing. The results of the Job Assessment

Worksheet should have thoroughly and clearly provided the following information:

- Job title

- Employee classification and skill level

- To whom the position reports

- Job summary—a brief description of essential responsibilities and what the position is meant to accomplish

- Major responsibilities and duties: list in order of importance the essential functions of the job; describe what must be accomplished, not how it must be done; include supervision or management responsibilities, quality and quantity standards. Normally, these are one-line descriptions starting with a verb such as *Directs, Manages, Performs* or *Operates.*

- Identify mental and physical essentials: These must be truly "essential" to performing the job to assure compliance with disability laws.

- Minimum requirements for education, experience, special skills and licenses or certifications required

- Indicate special equipment that may be used

- Working conditions should also be described

Job descriptions often focus heavily, if not exclusively, on minimum objective requirements, such as education and job experience. However, it is just as important to address the more subjective behavioral competencies essential to a job, such as flexibility, agility and strategic insight. An example: If you needed to let go of a manager who was not able to produce the required results because he was not a team player, being a team player should be listed on the job description. It should also be a basis for evaluation.

For consistency, adopt a standard format for the job description that addresses all of the critical elements. That will make it easy to use in hiring, development and employee evaluation, and provide clear communication among team members. We have evolved a format that accomplishes that purpose. It has been favorably received and utilized by our clients.

On the accompanying CD-ROM, we have included a sample job description for a customer service representative.

On the CD

Sample Job Description

It is our view that the clearly defined job description is essential in clarifying the roles and responsibilities of the position and in establishing standards of performance that everyone can understand and accept. It is important to remember that if things go wrong

—and they sometimes do—a clear, thoroughly discussed and acknowledged job description can prove invaluable in situations that could end up in a courtroom. Also know that a job description is the first place the courts will look when determining exempt or non-exempt status under the Fair Labor Standards Act (FLSA).

It is amazing to us that many companies fail to accurately define their organization and the positions within it. All too often, as we assist in the recruiting process, the first efforts are geared to filling this void. Over time, we have managed to create a large library of job descriptions for critical positions in the industries we support. We are now able to provide an added service for clients who may not be hiring, but who are striving to get organized.

STEP 2
DEFINE THE
PERSON

STEP 2: DEFINE THE PERSON

In **Step 1: Define the Job**, we described the process for determining the specifics of the job position and its functional requirements. These then became the basis for the written job description. When properly prepared, the job description thoroughly and clearly describes the major responsibilities and duties, the technical skills, and educational and experience qualifications required for the job as well as the working conditions that exist.

Now, in Step 2 of the hiring process, we introduce analytical tools to ensure that the staffing process brings in applicants who will have the right human behavioral characteristics to fit the requirements of your job and your team environment. These assessment tools should not be used to make the hiring decision for you; however, they will provide accurate and validated insights into a person's soft skills in terms of personality, understanding their work styles and identifying their work strengths. The assessment tools we recommend for determining one's soft skills also provide feedback on how well an individual will behave in varied circumstances and under certain conditions.

Often we find that businesses
hire for skills and fire for behaviors.

We, on the other hand, strongly recommend that you
hire for attitude and train for the skills.

In validating the success of our hiring process we have repeatedly demonstrated the value of knowing and understanding the personality of all members of the team and of all potential employees. Through many years of benchmarking top performers, we have created a clear understanding of the personalities that best fit certain positions. This ensures having a workable blend with the other team members.

Personality Profiling Based on the DISC System

In order to understand the importance of including behavioral analysis as part of our staffing process, it is important to understand personality profiling. There are many different personality profile assessments available today. We have researched and tested a vast majority of them, and have found the Thomas Personality Profiling System to be our number one choice. The Thomas System is based on the DISC methodology, which has proven to be extremely accurate and user-friendly. The results are easy to interpret and understand. A more important reason we highly recommend the Thomas System is because it is continually tested for reliability and validity. It also works well within the overall intention of the USA's Equal Employment Opportunity Commission (EEOC) guidelines and the Canadian Human Rights Act, which require that assessment instruments:

- Must be administered by qualified administrators.

- Are reliable and valid.

- Are unbiased and culturally fair.

- Have a job component that does not discriminate against candidates.

Brief History of the Psychology of Personal Profile Analysis

Early origins of the assessment theory stem from the work of Hippocrates (460 BC). His theory, known as Four Quadrant Behavior (4QB), emerged as a way of quantifying behavioral styles. Carl Gustav Jung (1920) used 4QB Theory to assess behavior in the workplace and introduced the dimensions of Extraversion and Introversion to the 4QB Model.

In 1928, Dr. William Moulton Marston, a Harvard professor, published the book *The Emotions of Normal People*. In it he described behavior in the workplace on two axes: passive vs. active response relative to a hostile or favorable environment. By placing these axes at right angles, four quadrants were formed with each circumscribing a behavioral pattern. He originally termed the four quadrants Dominance, Inducement, Submission and Compliance, or DISC Theory.

Dr. Marston's work has had a profound influence on theories such as Allport's Trait Measurement, Murray's Need Theory and Jackson's Personality Domains. The Five Factor Model (The Big Five) shows renewed interest in how parsimoniously measurements of personality functions may be described by reducing large inventories to five within-subject, possibly bi-polar dimensions.

In 1950, five psychologists from Harvard University, one of whom was Dr. Thomas Hendrickson, developed a psychometric instrument called the Personal Profile Analysis (PPA) based on Dr. Marston's theory. The PPA is a 24 item, ipsative instrument, which takes 10 to 15 minutes to complete. From the individual pattern of responses, a graphical representation of the degree of preferences for types of job behavior is given along four dimensions now called Dominance, Influence, Steadiness and Compliance. Written information about the significance of the profile is contained in an individual report generated from an extensive set of standard statements. These include commentary about likely work behavior, contexts for maximum job satisfaction and suggestions for questions to ask in the interview.

Read together with data about the person's previous work experience, qualifications, training and ability, the PPA can provide helpful understanding as to how an applicant copes with his/her environment and what his/her attitudes are likely to be at work. It also provides insight into possible performance in a particular function. Because it is an instrument that is gathering self-reported data, it is positive in nature and, on the whole, the resulting analysis is acceptable to the individual concerned.

The PPA is not a clinical instrument. It is a work-based assessment that enables organizations to use the system with other instruments and data to make more informed decisions regarding the compatibility of an individual with a particular function.

This brief history of the Personality Profiling System was drawn from the Thomas International Training Guide, "Increasing People Effectiveness."

Dr. Marston's Model of Behavior Chart

BEHAVIOR
Active (Externalizer)

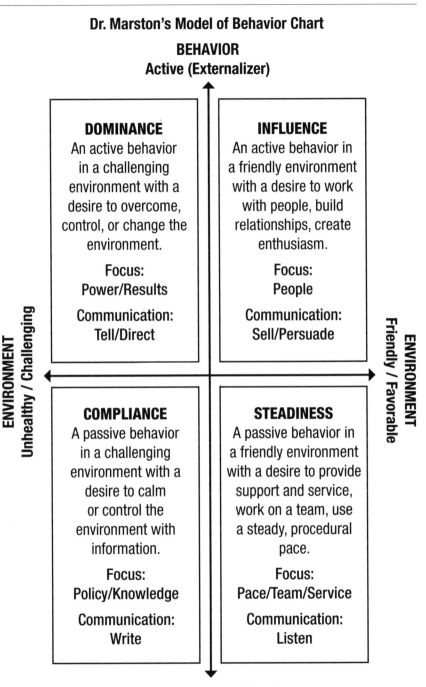

ENVIRONMENT
Unhealthy / Challenging

ENVIRONMENT
Friendly / Favorable

DOMINANCE
An active behavior in a challenging environment with a desire to overcome, control, or change the environment.

Focus:
Power/Results

Communication:
Tell/Direct

INFLUENCE
An active behavior in a friendly environment with a desire to work with people, build relationships, create enthusiasm.

Focus:
People

Communication:
Sell/Persuade

COMPLIANCE
A passive behavior in a challenging environment with a desire to calm or control the environment with information.

Focus:
Policy/Knowledge

Communication:
Write

STEADINESS
A passive behavior in a friendly environment with a desire to provide support and service, work on a team, use a steady, procedural pace.

Focus:
Pace/Team/Service

Communication:
Listen

Passive (Internalizer)
BEHAVIOR

Thomas Personality Profiling System

The keystone output of the Thomas System is the Personal Profile Analysis (PPA). The PPA uses the DISC methodology to identify the human behavioral characteristics within a person. Validation and reliability studies have repeatedly demonstrated the accuracy of the PPA when properly administered.

Each person has a unique personality profile. But just as William Marston illustrated, there are only four characteristics to consider. It has also been shown that each combination of the characteristics identifies a behavior pattern that may be best suited for specific job assignments. The recognition of the pattern and the probability of job suitability have made the PPA a logical tool for assisting in:

- Developing people
- Building teams
- Identifying strengths and limitations
- Recruiting and selecting the right person the first time
- Resolving conflict
- Performance appraisals
- Developing/coaching management skills
- Identifying training needs
- Succession planning
- Identifying leadership potential
- Benchmarking performance
- Mentoring
- Career mapping
- Motivating employees

When used in this manner, the PPA produces results that are measurable through reduced turnover, increased motivation and productivity, better customer service and more cohesive teams.

The foundation of the PPA is a set of graphs that portray the relative values of the DISC behavioral characteristics. Specifically, the PPA graphs address the self-image: how the person really is; the work mask: how the person adjusts for the work environment; and behavior under stress: what changes take place in a stressful environment. The PPA identifies the personality traits and preferences that characterize a person's actions and reactions and highlights special talents. Each personality has its own points of reference, its own values and behavior patterns.

On the following page is a chart that provides an overview of the behavioral characteristics. Use this chart as a quick reference guide to review the results of a completed personal profile.

Behavioral Characteristics Overview Chart

	DOMINANCE (D)	INFLUENCE (I)	STEADINESS (S)	COMPLIANCE (C)
HIGH Work Strengths	• Assertive • Competitive • Direct • Driving • Forceful • Inquisitive • Self-starter	• Communicative • Friendly • Influential • Persuasive • Positive • Verbal	• Amiable • Deliberate • Dependable • Good Listener • Kind • Persistent	• Accurate • Careful • Compliant • Logical • Perfectionist • Precise
LOW Support Factors	• Consultative • Non-demanding • Cautious • Conservative • Mild	• Probing • Reflective • Serious • Factual • Logical	• Active • Alert • Demonstrative • Mobile • Restless	• Firm • Independent • Persistent • Strong-willed • Stubborn
Focus	• Power	• People	• Pace	• Policy
Communication Style	• Tell	• Sell	• Listen	• Write
Motivators	• Tangible Goals	• Recognition	• Security • Team Inclusion	• Policy and Information
Fears	• Failure	• Rejection	• Insecurity • Exclusion	• Conflict • Chaos
Question	• What	• Who	• Why	• How
Leadership Style	• Authoritarian	• Democratic	• Procedural	• Knowledge based

⬜ = Based on high characteristics

Copyright © 2006 Thomas International USA Inc.

Human Job Analysis

Once it became apparent that behavioral fit was dependent on both the specific demands of the job and also the culture within the team, it was only logical that the DISC methodology needed a tool to help hiring managers predict the right behaviors that their team needed. The outcome of that need was the Human Job Analysis (HJA), the tool we recommend to use in **Step 2: Define the Person.**

The HJA adds structure to the selection process and ensures that candidates are assessed against job criteria. The HJA identifies the "ideal" human behavioral characteristics within a function. The creation of the HJA is a critical early step in the hiring process.

Just as individuals have different characteristics, so each position requires individuals with unique characteristics to best accomplish the tasks and ensure greater success.

On the accompanying CD-ROM you will find a .pdf of the HJA form. Print it out and use it to evaluate any current positions for which you are hiring.

HJA Form

In a series of 24 questions, at least two to four people who are familiar with the function should reach consensus in evaluating each competency for its relevance in a particular position. The more people involved in the creation, the more objective it will be. There should be considerable discussion about each of the questions to make sure that there is, in fact, agreement on the results.

Once a job has been rated and the results validated by comparing them to successful performers, a benchmark of success criteria is established. The result of this process is a profile graph that is related to the same four DISC characteristics. This benchmark becomes the objective standard against which people currently in the role—or future candidates interested in it—can be compared.

Sample Results of the Completed HJA Form

The completed graph should have factors above and below the midline.

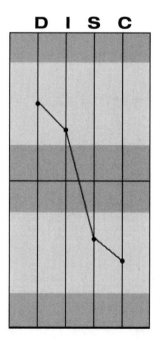

D I S C

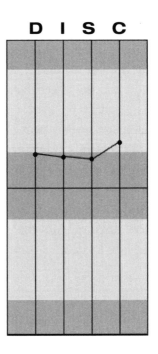

When all of the factors are above the midline, the importance of all DISC factors has been overstated (over-shift).

D I S C

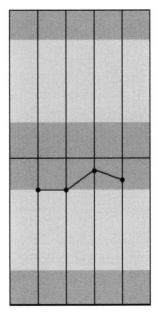

When the factors are all below the midline, the importance of all DISC factors has been understated (under-shift).

Whether the factors have been overstated or understated, the midline must be adjusted to weight the graph correctly. To do so, move the midline so that it intersects the graph midway between the highest and the lowest factors.

Shown here are several example profiles of proven top performers in key roles within a business or organization. It is important to note that although these examples are of top performers, they may not work as well in your culture or with your team. That is why we recommend an HJA be completed for your particular function and that the predominant ideal behavioral characteristics be defined for every position that needs to be filled.

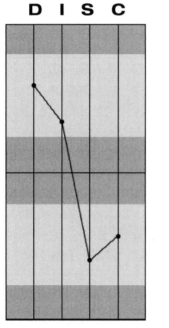

Manager

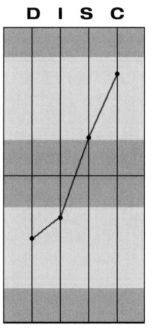

Production

D I S C

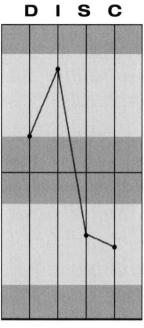

Sales

On the accompanying CD-ROM you will find a .pdf of the HJA form to define the personality for your particular position. You will also find classic profiles for a customer service representative to use as examples.

The Position Is Defined

Once both the job description and the HJA are completed, you have defined the optimal combination of skills, experience, education and personality. Now you are ready to begin the search for your Grade AA talent!

STEP 3: RECRUIT

*Recruiting today has become more difficult and
potentially more expensive than ever.*

Judging by the continuing use of "Now Hiring" signs on display,
it seems that many companies are dependent on long-standing
methods for getting the word out to hire help. It may be entirely
possible that the applicant of your dreams will walk through the
door as soon as you have defined the job and the person you want.
However, that is highly unlikely, so this step in the hiring process
requires you to get the word out. This, like all of the other steps to
staffing success, must be well thought out. Your goal is not to get
flooded with tons of paper, but to get a good selection of qualified
applicants. The methods that you use and the advertisements
you create have to reach the right people, make them want to be
considered, and also make them want to work for your company.

Recruiting today is more difficult and expensive than ever. Depending on where you live, the pool of candidates may be small or mostly
unacceptable. When unemployment is around 5%, it means the
candidate pool consists mostly of the "unemployables." In 2009,
when unemployment approached 10%, it was still difficult to find
"qualified" employees. Attempts to find any applicants under these
circumstances may take a long time to produce the right results. This
points out the need to plan your recruiting campaign carefully.

Also consider the difference between active job seekers and passive
job seekers. Active job seekers are just that; they are actively searching
all media sources to find the positions of their dreams. Passive job
seekers are not really looking, but might still be interested in the
right opportunity. A common perception is that the passive job
seeker is a better performer than an active one, so your recruiting
methods need to reach the passive job seeker.

Recruiting Resources

Once you decide to recruit, there are many different resources that you can use, and you may need to try several to find the best candidates. There are obvious considerations of cost and the ability to reach the right pool of candidates. In addition to giving careful thought to the methods to be used, you should continually reevaluate them based on the quantity and quality of the responses and the economic times. Approximately half of all hires come about through internal postings or referrals. Job boards represent the next best option, while ads in newspapers are only marginally better than a "Now Hiring" sign in the window.

Following is a discussion of various methods to help you decide on the best approach for you.

1. **Print Media:** Often referred to as the "Pay and Pray" method. You pay to run the ad, and then pray that someone qualified responds.

    a. Newspaper Advertising: Classified ads are still an effective way to reach active job seekers. However, classified ads have never been the best way to reach passive candidates. The difficulty is that the cost of newspaper advertising may force you to limit the size of the ad or the frequency that it runs. As a result, it can be a matter of timing or luck that will enable you to find the right person for the position. For positions that are temporary, part time, or seasonal, the newspaper is still a viable recruiting resource.

    Newspapers have recognized that the Internet represents the best tool, so many newspapers will also post the ad in their online newspaper and run it for much longer periods of time with just a small charge over the cost of the newspaper ad. In some cases, the newspapers are linked to online sourcces like CareerBuilder or Monster so you get the advantage of their job postings for a lower fee than the regular CareerBuilder or Monster posting. However, the combination of the newspaper and Internet ad is more costly than going straight to the Internet. The value of the newspaper posting would have to be evaluated based on your position and your market.

We recommend placing a small ad in the newspaper that minimally describes the vacancy and provides a link or Internet address to a site where lots of information can be found. It doesn't have to be your online newspaper or CareerBuilder or Monster; it could be the employment page on your own company site. Savvy job seekers will go to your site anyway to check you out; you might as well help them find it quickly.

Customer Service / Account Representative

(XYZ Company) seeks energetic, customer focused person. Exp a plus. Great compensation & benefits.

For more info visit:

www.xyzcompany.com

The newspaper will give you the link to CareerBuilder or Monster. Then you will be able to access the position description and modify it to include all of the pertinent information.

b. Newsletters: There are profession-related newsletters and periodicals you might want to advertise in along with newsletters of different organizations within your community.

c.   **College Newspapers:** If a college student or upcoming graduate would be a good candidate, place your ad in a college or university paper. Most times these ads are at no cost. It is especially important to work with those colleges that have curricula matching your professional needs and skills. Many colleges do have vocational training that can be a valuable source of applicants.

2. **Employment, Recruiting or Staffing Agency:** Outside employment firms are also a good source for recruiting. However, when approaching such a firm, it is important to be aware there are different types of agencies. You will have to determine if their specialty fits your needs. It is also very important that you understand their fee structure and the terms of the agreement prior to signing up for this type of program.

Although an agency may have the ability to send candidates your way, it does not mean that these candidates will be right. You will still have to conduct the remainder of the steps recommended in the hiring process to ensure the person is the right fit for your position and your organization. Only a few employment agencies do any of the necessary legwork to qualify applicants. That responsibility still falls on the hiring manager.

Bringing on a candidate with a "temp-to-perm" agreement is another option to consider. That offers the opportunity to evaluate the person's ability and fit prior to offering him or her a permanent position. Once again, although the person may appear to be working out just fine, you must still conduct the remainder of the steps to ensure you have the right fit.

3. **Recruit Within:** Recruit your own employees before someone else does. Many companies find internal recruiting is their most successful method for finding both active and passive applicants. Post jobs internally before going outside

the company. Give current employees the opportunity to interview for the position. Even if they are not qualified for the position, it creates a more positive environment because they feel good having an opportunity to interview before you bring in outsiders. You may be surprised to find qualified people who are interested in changing positions within your own company. Post your positions on an employment opportunities page on your website. Whether you intend to hire within, use referrals as discussed below, or advertise outside the company, your website is critical to the process. Techno-savvy applicants research prospective employers and can either get excited by what they see on your site or be turned off by it.

4. **Employee Referral Programs:** One tried-and-true recruiting method that strong companies swear by is getting referrals from their own top employees. A well-thought-out program tied to incentives for referrals and retention can turn employees into "headhunters" for the company. These contacts between your employees and their friends and relatives are an excellent way to search out passive job seekers. Remember, it is easier to get employees to refer friends and family members when they believe the company is a good place to work. Also, they will be selective about whom they recruit, only referring friends they think will be an asset rather than a burden to the company. Typically, an incentive includes a cash payment made to the employee who gave the referral once the new hire has been on the job 90 days or six months. Obviously, the critical nature of the position may motivate you to offer even greater incentives.

On the accompanying CD-ROM you will find an Employee Referral Form.

5. **Customer Referrals:** Your customers may be looking for a career change, or they may know someone who would make an

excellent employee. Get the word out to customers on statements and flyers, on your website or using on-hold telephone messages. As noted earlier, put the "Now Hiring" sign out and people who visit your facility will get the word out, especially when they have a good relationship with the company. Finding a top performer takes all of the ingenuity available.

Employee Referral Form

6. **Vendor Referrals:** It's a good idea to let your vendors know you are looking to fill a position. Since they are in the field, they are often the first to know about a good employee who has been recently laid off. They may also know about good employees who are unhappy with their present positions.

7. **Public Appearances and Networking:** Develop and maintain a high profile and positive reputation in your

community. Spreading the word about your hiring needs is always a good idea.

8. **The School Connection:** One of the reasons we do not have students coming out of school eager to join specific professions is because they "don't know what they don't know." Be proactive in spreading the word to the schools about what your industry has to offer. Here are some ways to do this:

- Be available to speak at career-day functions. Schools are always looking for business owners and professionals to be speakers at these events.

- Establish an internship or mentor program for students.

- Provide tours so schools can bring their students through.

- Junior Achievement programs and Scouts are always looking to find out more about businesses in their neighborhoods. Invite them in for tours and show them around. Get them excited at an early age and they will be interested when you need them.

9. **University Career Counseling Centers:** Most universities and colleges have career counseling centers that help students and graduates find part-time and full-time employment. Making them aware of your job needs could provide access to another candidate pool.

10. **Welcome Wagon:** If you have Welcome Wagon services in your area, provide them with information about your need to hire. Their flyers go to residents with spouses and relatives who may be looking for jobs in your area.

11. **Online Ad Placement Options:** Online recruiting has become the most popular employment tool for companies of all sizes. Not only do the ads run longer at lower cost than in print advertising, but many of the sites incorporate tools

to help prescreening and validating of applicants. While there may be some reasons to pick particular Internet hosting sites based on regional location or industry specific, once placed on the Internet, the opportunity reaches a larger audience. It is not unusual to get resumes from all across the country and even from foreign countries. While out-of-state applicants may be looking for relocation assistance, many candidates may already be planning to move to a new location for a wide variety of reasons, making them willing to relocate on their own for the right career opportunity.

An advantage of many Internet job boards is their use of auto-responders to communicate with applicants. This puts courtesy in the hiring process. If you choose a job board that includes this feature, don't just rely on the default format of the auto-responder, but customize it to fit your company and provide the response that you want the applicant to receive.

Below we have listed several ideas for Internet postings. These only represent a small sampling of the numerous job boards available. While we believe these sites will give you adequate resources to choose from, also seek out additional sites related to your specific industry, association or location.

a. **Your Company Website:** We recommend you create an Employment Opportunities or Career page on your company website and keep it as a permanent page on your site. This will allow you to immediately post any position you may have available. It also gives you the ability to make the ad as lengthy as you like and post it for as long as you want. Not only do potential applicants find detailed information about the position, they can also find out about the company at the same time. The more informative and impressive your website, the greater chance you have to encourage top-performing applicants to apply. Conversely a poorly designed website could discourage them.

If you do not have any immediate openings, we still recommend you keep the Employment Opportunities page handy and continually recruit. You can state something like, "While we may not have any immediate openings, we are always looking for good people to join us as we grow our business. Please send an email to Jerry@CompanyName .com along with your resume. Thank you for your interest in our company."

b. **RegionalHelpWanted.com:** The RegionalHelpWanted website has city-specific sites throughout the U.S. and Canada. It offers online ad postings for 30 days at rates that are usually less than national sites. Check the home page to find the particular site that exists for the city or region in which you are recruiting. Then find out how active the particular site is in your location before you place the ad.

c. **Monster.com:** As the world's leading career site, Monster has more traffic, more resumes and more effective ways to help you target and search than any other online hiring resource. Ads on Monster run for 60 days and can be easily renewed. They also provide the opportunity to go in and make changes to the ad in order to make it more attractive or to clarify information for applicants.

Monster also allows you to create prescreening questions that must be answered before applicants can submit their resumes. It has filtering tools built into the job posting so you can quickly narrow the candidate pool to the most qualified candidates.

We highly recommend you add the prescreening questions to any site that provides that option. We will address the use of prescreening in more depth in Step 4. The sample prescreening questions you will see on the accompanying CD-ROM can easily be adapted for the online prescreening.

Be sure to include these at the time you post the ad. If you attempt to add them later, it could cost more.

On Monster you may also purchase access to its resume pool to proactively pursue potential candidates. Contact Monster directly to find the different pricing structures for this feature. Additionally, Monster offers a variety of packages that will significantly lower your cost per ad.

d. CareerBuilder.com: For some time, CareerBuilder has been a very viable online site for job postings. CareerBuilder is continually adding enhancements so it can be even more competitive with Monster. CareerBuilder has become very aggressive advertising on TV so that, more and more, it is becoming the first choice for job seekers. The real advantage that CareerBuilder provided early was aligning with local newspapers throughout the country. If you find this to be the case in your area, special rates apply to run both a short newspaper ad for one or two days and a full online ad for 30 days.

For example, the newspaper ad will run for two days (Sunday and Wednesday) but the online version of the ad will run for 30 days. Once the ad is placed in the newspaper, you can get a link from CareerBuilder that enables you to go in and modify the ad. It lets you add as many words as you want to fully describe the position and the company. You can also modify the ad anytime during its 30-day run. Recently, Monster has established links with newspapers and now offers the same capability.

CareerBuilder also enables you to add prescreening questions like Monster does. However, its postings only run for 30 days even though the cost is very similar to Monster. It has packages that can significantly reduce the cost per ad if you are doing extensive hiring. It also offers resume searching.

e. **TG & Associates' Job Board:** We created our own Internet job board on our website at tgassociates.com for businesses that are not able to (or do not want to) post ads on their website. We often encounter hiring managers who want to replace employees, but do not want to terminate them until suitable replacements have been found. They also do not want to let current employees know they are in danger of being replaced, so the ad must be confidential. Our job board offers the opportunity to run blind ads that describe positions without identifying the company. By using the combination ad discussed earlier, a company can put a short ad about a position being available in the local newspaper and refer applicants to TG & Associates' Job Board. Our job board is supported by its own email system so all correspondence with applicants remains discreet until an interview is set up.

f. **Craigslist.org:** Another great website for job postings
    is Craigslist, a recent entry into the Internet job boards.
    This service, which is based in San Francisco, offers great
    opportunities for posting jobs available around the country.
    It is a very responsive website that is currently offering free
    job postings in many cities. It does charge for ads in some
    locations, but it is significantly less than many of the other
    job boards. Go to craigslist.org to check if your city is
    listed. The posting process is easy and quick. Because it is
    new, there may be fewer responses than the other boards,
    but it is quickly gaining recognition.

g. **Niche Websites:** There are a vast number of other Internet job
    boards. Many of these cater to specific industries or speciality
    disciplines. Check to see if any of these sites fit your industry
    or the specific job function that you need to fill.

Tailoring Your Classified Ad

While the location of your Internet posting is important to your
recruiting, the words of the ad will be critical to attracting the
perfect candidate. On the Internet, you have all the room you
need to convey the perfect message, so make it inspirational,
motivational and industry specific. Hiring the right personality for
the position is such a critical component for job success that all
ads should be written to attract the right personality. Be creative
to engage, inform and excite the right applicant. Your ad needs to
stand out from the crowd if you intend to recruit the best.

Within your ad, it is important to include detailed company
information such as services offered and interesting facts about your
location. This information is especially critical to attract candidates
who might be interested in relocating to your particular area. Give
them enough information so they know your company is in a place
where they want to work and can count on for a career.

Refer to the job description you created in **Step 1: Define the Job** and insert the main duties and responsibilities of the position. Be very clear about the qualifications you are looking for in your applicants. Also describe the working conditions along with benefits and compensation information. Make sure you clearly state in the ad how you want applicants to contact you. There is one thing we have learned. They will figure out who you are and contact you even if it is not the way you specify.

Applicant Tracking Systems

If you expect to do a lot of hiring, you might want to invest in an Applicant Tracking System (ATS). Then you can arrange to have all of the applications routed through the ATS. These have built-in tools that will let you do even more prescreening and enable you to track the status all of the applicants. Many include auto responders to let applicants know you received their resumes and will get back to them as soon as you can. They also can provide libraries of email formats to seek out other information and notify applicants that they didn't make the grade. These tools allow you to put both control and courtesy into your recruiting process.

Why All the Fuss?

This process is all about finding Grade AA talent. Clearly if you are willing to settle for just a warm body, you don't need to expend this much effort. But if you want employees who will be key elements in your business, you need to understand the ways and means of recruiting and do it right. If you create the right ad and post it appropriately, you will find a better pool of candidates that you can move to the next step in the process.

On the accompanying CD-ROM you will find a sample ad for a customer service representative suitable for Internet posting. You will also find a Classifed Ad Placement Request Form and a Classified Ad Placement Log.

STEP 4
PRESCREEN

STEP 4: PRESCREEN

Prescreening must be designed and conducted to quickly
weed out the applicants who are not viable for the position.

Depending on the situation in your area and the position that was advertised, the degree of response to your ads may vary from a handful to hundreds of resumes. Many times applicants will respond in the manner you defined in the ad, but they may also respond directly in a separate email if they have learned your email address. With today's technology, it is very rare that you will ever get a letter with an attached resume via the U.S. postal system. But by whatever means you receive them, the fact is that many of the resumes will never fit your need.

This step of the hiring process is designed to help you quickly screen through the pile of paper and select the applicants you want to move through the process. Remember, it is the applicant's responsibility to prove that he or she meets the stated requirements. You spent a considerable amount of time carefully defining the job, and this is not the time to start settling for applicants who clearly do not possess the needed skills. This is not a selection step: rather it is an elimination step.

This step really involves three levels of prescreening. The first level is the careful scrutiny of the resume itself. Don't jump to conclusions over a beautifully written and printed resume. Remember, applicants can work with services that can turn a pig's ear into a silk purse. Read between the lines and make sure that you do a thorough job of comparing the resume to the position description and the requirements that you placed in your ad. Conversely, don't get turned off by a resume that comes across email in a disjointed manner. We have seen some beautifully prepared resumes decimated by the scanning and/or the online insertion tools. You need to focus on the words, not the appearance. The following are some items to watch for in reviewing resumes.

Skills/Experience

- Job skills you require
- Directly related experience
- Transferable skills

Good Signs

- Measurable results
- Promotions or increased pay at one company
- Multiple jobs within the same company
- Rehired by the same company
- Education, certificates, training
- Good writing skills

Red Flags or Warning Signs

- Past experience unrelated to position applied for
- Unexplained time gaps between jobs
- Previous employment dates that list only the year
- Inconsistent information, vague information, or areas omitted
- Description of job duties not consistent with job title
- Supervisors' names and past employment missing
- Job hopping or career jumps
- Short tenure in positions without logical reasons
- Unclear career goals
- Spelling errors and typos

The next level of prescreening involves the use of a written questionnaire that includes specific things of importance to you in selecting the right person. One of the valuable features on Monster, CareerBuilder and ATS is the ability to insert in the posting a series of prescreening questions that applicants are asked to complete in addition to providing their resumes. This new tool even allows you to weight the value of each of the prescreening questions. The job board or ATS will tally the results and give you the total score in the header of the response from the applicant. If you have properly prepared and weighted your questions, you can decide to quickly rule out the applicants who score less than a 50. While we may look at resumes that score around 50, we are rather skeptical of resumes that score a perfect 100. Just as with any other part of the application process, there is no protection against applicants who lie or exaggerate their capabilities. In **Step 6: Structured Interview**, we will provide guidelines for the questions you can or cannot ask. Those same guidelines apply to the prescreening. There are areas that are off limits under the EEOC or ADA provisions. Ask the wrong questions and you may be accused of discrimination.

When you prepare questions for online prescreening, consider the following guidelines;

- Use open-ended questions that require a written statement. These not only provide useful information, they help evaluate the applicant's skills at written communication.

- Ask applicants to provide information about their background and experience related to critical job functions.

- Ask questions that get a sense of the applicants' career goals and areas of their work experience they preferred.

If you choose to use another method of advertising that does not provide online prescreening questions, then we strongly recommend you email the prescreening questions to those applicants whose resumes indicate potential for a good fit. This step will enable you to cull through the candidates fast and obtain preliminary information easily. Review the responses just as thoroughly as you did the resumes using the same guidelines to find the good and the bad. But more importantly, look at the specific responses to the questions that were very important to you. If the responses are unsatisfactory, then it is time to move on to other candidates.

The third level of prescreening is the telephone prescreen, which focuses on key aspects of the position. It is another opportunity to make sure that additional testing and interviewing is only done on the qualified candidates that show potential. There will be unexpected opportunities to do the telephone prescreening. Some applicants will call and request more information about the job. If they call, be prepared to do the telephone prescreen. It is often difficult to connect with applicants who are working, so it can be extremely beneficial to be able to act when the opportunity strikes. If they follow a normal routine and forward a resume, then evaluate it and the written prescreening results first. If it looks like a fit, then plan for the telephone prescreening. Before you make any contact with the applicants to do a telephone prescreen, have a list of questions prepared. Be ready to ask all the candidates the same questions so you get an apples-to-apples comparison.

In conducting the telephone prescreen, it is important to respect the privacy of the candidates in these ways:

- Avoid mentioning the reason for your call until the candidate is on the phone.
- Determine if you've picked a convenient time for the candidate to talk. If not, make arrangements to call at a better time.
- Decide if calling at home after work hours is the best approach.

The goal of the telephone prescreen is to devote a minimal amount of time to asking several significant questions that will quickly identify the suitability of a candidate. Like any step of the hiring process, the prescreening must be planned well and you must be in charge. Document the answers that you are given. As you listen to the responses, also listen for things such as the tone of voice and enthusiasm of the responder. In particular, if the job description calls for being on the telephone, pay attention to the applicant's phone etiquette.

Here are 18 recommended prescreening questions that you should ask all applicants. Their responses should be recorded. If at any time a response does not fit what you are looking for, then it is appropriate to thank the candidates for their time and inform them that they are not a match for the position. Also note that these particular questions can be used when tailoring the prescreening questions that you will use on CareerBuilder, Monster, or any Internet site that allows you to have prescreening questions answered when the candidates submit their resume.

Recommended Prescreening Questions

1. Why are you interested in this position?
2. This is a full-time (part-time) position. Is this acceptable to you?
3. Are there any days or hours you cannot work?
4. Are you currently employed?
   a. If yes, why are you leaving your current job?
   b. If no, when did you last work and why did you leave?
5. Have you ever been fired from a job or asked to leave? If yes, please explain.
6. When would you be able to start work?
7. What are some things you would like to avoid in a job? Why?

8. Will you grant us your permission to contact your current employer now to verify information?

9. If not now, may we have your permission to contact your current employer if you are offered a position?

10. Will you give us permission to contact previous employers?

11. What will your references tell us about you?

12. What are your income expectations from this job?

13. Will you follow a dress code?

14. What skills and strengths can you bring to this position?

15. What gives you the greatest satisfaction?

16. What frustrates you the most?

17. Based on what you know about the position, in what areas do you think you will need to develop yourself to be ready for it?

18. Is there anything else you think we need to know at this time?

In your evaluation of the resume and the conduct of prescreening, be sure to stay focused on the job itself.

- Determine the requirements for the position and if this candidate can fulfill them.

- Treat all candidates consistently.

- Be aware of the Anti-Discrimination Guidelines and make sure your prescreening questions comply.

 You will find Anti-Discrimination Guidelines and a Telephone Prescreening Form for a customer service representative position on the accompanying CD-ROM.

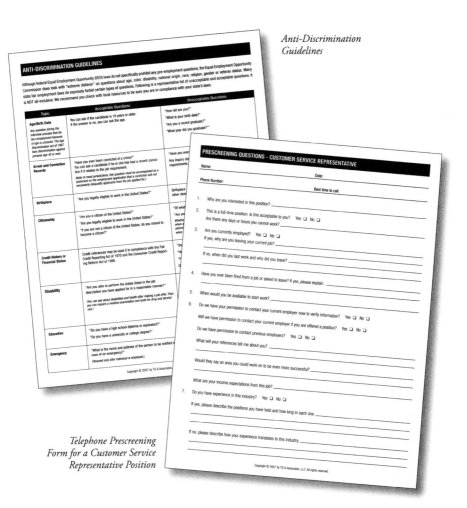

*Anti-Discrimination
Guidelines*

*Telephone Prescreening
Form for a Customer Service
Representative Position*

Do not plan on bringing in every applicant for a full interview. That is a waste of your time and theirs. Use the prescreening to eliminate applicants who are not suitable and also to rank those who appear suitable at this point. Do not bring in candidates for the structured interview who did not satisfy your prescreen in the mistaken belief that the prescreen did not catch the real person. We recommend you use prescreening to "smoke out" salary issues early. You want to know the potential for creating a win-win situation. If the salary expectations are out of your budget or unrealistic for the skills and experience of the applicant, then save everybody's time and end the call.

One of the key threads you will see in our hiring process is the need for checking and testing. Prescreening is only the first phase of that process. Later we will look at the structured interview, competency testing, personality profiling, and reference and background checking to find out everything we can about the applicant before an offer is made. The recommended checks and all aspects of those checks are important. Get in the habit of finding out everything you can during every opportunity that comes up.

If you continue the hiring process with specific candidates and invite them in for an interview, it is important to advise them you will be contacting references, conducting background checks, requiring drug and medical tests, and administering additional assessments as part of the interviewing process. Having this information up front gives them the option of continuing with the process or bowing out. For example, some applicants may know they cannot pass a drug test so they will choose not to continue with the interview process. Other applicants know that something questionable may show up in their background check. They may opt to share it with you prior to the interview or elect to bow out.

If you decide for any reason not to bring in an applicant for an interview, you should let that person know. It is best to inform the candidate in a timely and professional manner so that both of you can get on to other things. Here are two opportunities for informing candidates that they are not a fit for the position:

1. Based solely on reviewing a resume and the submitted prescreening questionnaire, you may decide that an applicant is not a good fit. As this point, send an email, letter or postcard thanking the person for being interested and saying he or she is not a match for the position. Since you did not actually talk to the candidate, it is not required to make this type of acknowledgement, but do it out of courtesy and to make a positive impression about your

company. Based on an initial telephone prescreen, you may determine right away that the candidate is not a fit. As already mentioned, it is appropriate to politely end the prescreening session as soon as you decide he or she is not a fit for the position. Say thank you for taking the time to talk to you. Then say that, based on the preliminary conversation, you do not think you have a good fit.

2. Once you have made it to **Step 9: Hiring Decision** and selected the right person, out of courtesy, call, email or send a letter or postcard to all candidates who had been verbally contacted and prescreened. Let them know they did not get the position and personally thank them for their interest and their time. Say that you have chosen another candidate who was better qualified for the position.

On the accompanying CD-ROM you will find a sample letter of non-selection and a sample letter of non-selection following prescreening.

Sample Letter of Non-Selection

Do not lower the bar.

We do not want to sound like a broken record, but each step in the hiring process is vital to the success of hiring the right person the first time. Do not neglect any of the steps and do not allow applicants to pass on to the next step of the hiring process if they do not meet the specific criteria for the job requirements.

It will cost you in the end.

STEP 5
EMPLOYMENT
APPLICATION

STEP 5: EMPLOYMENT APPLICATION

We have a resume and we have done the prescreening;
why do we need to have the candidate complete
an application form?

We get this question often from managers and owners who see the application as just more bureaucracy. The fact is that the employment application remains one of the most indispensable tools in the hiring process. The application is designed to capture the minimum information necessary to assist with the hiring decision. To accept less (perhaps just a resume) from some applicants not only affects your ability to do an apples-to-apples comparison, but if you have only some candidates (those without resumes, for example) complete the application, your action could also be construed as discriminatory.

Sure, some of the data requested on the application will be redundant to that contained on a resume, but here are five reasons why a completed and signed employment application is important.

1. The application form is a legal document. When completed and signed by the applicant, the application form asserts the truth and the accuracy of the information provided. Studies have shown that most resumes contain some untruths. If the applicant provides untruthful information regarding past employment history, education, or credentials in the applicant's own writing on the signed application form, it can serve as evidence to support a termination for falsifying employment information.

    Since the application is a legal document and could be needed in a future court action, do not make any notes on it. Even innocent comments could be construed as discriminatory. Do not fill in any missing information for the applicant. The document must be completely in the applicant's handwriting. If you feel compelled to make comments on the application form, do them on a separate sheet of paper or on Post-it notes.

2. The application form serves as a consistent tool for measuring applicants. Using a standard format makes it easier to compare the credentials of all the applicants against each other.

*Employment
Application*

3. The application brings standardization to the process. While a resume serves as a marketing tool for candidates to present their best side, the application objectively presents candidates in a more sterile fashion. You may also see that the information provided on the resume and on the application are sometimes different. When this happens, it should raise a red flag and trigger further examination.

4. The application provides additional help in prescreening applicants. For example, it can indicate spelling and grammar issues that are not present in the resume, which is often professionally prepared.

5. The application form should also include language that advises the applicant there will be both reference and background checks and employment is at-will and can be terminated at any time. The applicant's signature on the form gives you the authority to make reference checks immediately. However, a separate release form is required for the background check.

The fact that the application form is a legal document also carries with it the obligation to comply with federal and state legislation, which is intended to ensure fair and non-discriminatory hiring. As a hiring manager, you are entitled to information needed to make a good decision. However, there are many questions that cannot be asked. The rule of thumb is to not request any information that does not directly relate to the qualifications for the position as defined in the job description.

When determining if your employment application is EEOC compliant, refer to the Anti-Discrimination Guidelines on pages 89–93 or the accompanying CD-ROM. The same rules apply when verbally asking for information as they do for gathering information from a candidate in a written manner.

On the accompanying CD-ROM you will also find a copy of the Anti-Discrimination Guidelines.

Besides ensuring that the employment application itself does not ask for information that may be discriminatory, it is important to include a statement on the employment application that all employment relationships are "at-will." It must be clear that either party may terminate the employment relationship for any reason or for no reason at any time.

Screening the Application

In **Step 4: Prescreen**, we discussed the three levels of prescreening. The employment application gives us still another level. Check first to see if the applicant has the core qualifications as you defined them in the job description. Then move to more specific hiring criteria. Remember, the goal is to make sure applicants fit your preset criteria. It is great when they hit them all, but usually you will find a gap between the qualifications and the criteria. The issue then is to determine if the gap can be filled by training. If the criteria are not met and you are not comfortable that training can fix the shortcoming, move on to other applicants. This is one more time in the process when we strongly recommend that you *not* lower the bar. The goal is to continually weed out those who do not warrant the time involved in further evaluation.

Just as in reviewing the resume, watch for the following warning signs when screening the employment application:

Red Flags or Warning Signs
- Past experience unrelated to position applied for
- Unexplained time gaps between jobs
- Previous employment dates that list only the year
- Inconsistent information, vague information, or areas omitted

- Description of job duties not consistent with job title
- Supervisors' names and past employment missing
- Job hopping or career jumps
- Short tenure in positions without logical reasons
- Unclear career goals
- Spelling errors and typos
- Application not filled out completely, sloppy or not legible
- Lack of valid reason for leaving other jobs
- Information doesn't match with the resume or prescreening questions already answered

Good Signs

- Measurable results
- Promotions or increased pay at one company
- Multiple jobs within the same company
- Rehired by the same company
- Education, certificates, training
- Good writing skills

The employment application is a required step in the hiring process because:

1. It is a tremendous tool to assist in additional prescreening.
2. It is signed and dated by the employee and therefore it becomes a legal document.

Do not ever proceed with hiring without having a completed application. Always keep the information for future reference should any issues arise. This is true even for applicants you do not hire in case issues of employment discrimination come up.

On the CD

On the accompanying CD-ROM you will find an Employment Application and a Driver Application Form that we use and recommend.

DRIVER APPLICATION FORM

Driver Application Form

The Driver Application Form supplements the Employment Application Form and should be given to every applicant who will be driving for company business. Once you make a hiring decision and the individual will be driving for company business (e.g., delivery driver, outside sales person), then your insurance company should be notified so all of their documentation is completed and you will have adequate coverage and protection.

Notice that once the applicant has signed the "read, date and sign" section of the employment application, you will have the necessary authorization to conduct reference checks. These actions will be discussed in **Step 8: Reference Check**. Remember that you will need a separate release form for the background check, which is discussed in **Step 11: Final Checks.**

Record Retention Requirements

It is a federal legal requirement that employment applications received be retained for one full year from the date received. Employers generally keep applications as a part of any employee's personnel file. "No-hire" applications should be retained for a one-year minimum period, according to the Fair Labor Standards Act (FLSA).

On the accompanying CD-ROM you will find a link to the FLSA.

STEP 6
STRUCTURED
INTERVIEW

STEP 6: STRUCTURED INTERVIEW

Interviewing is an art. Properly conducted, an interview enables the hiring manager to determine the essential information he or she needs to select the candidate who will be a top performer. Proper conduct also means avoiding any questions that could be construed as discriminatory under state or federal employment law.

The first few steps of the hiring process involved a lot of communication between the hiring manager and the applicant over the Internet, email and phone. Now we are ready to move forward to the first actual meeting between the hiring manager and the applicant to further evaluate the fit of the applicant to the open position. While we often expect that the applicant may be nervous about the interview, the fact is that hiring managers are also nervous about the interview. It is a critical step in the potential relationship between employer and employee. Interviewing does not come naturally to everyone who may be involved in the interview process. Each person conducting an interview must be properly prepared and informed of the results of the hiring process to this point. This preparation will increase the effectiveness of the actual interview.

This step is called the structured interview because it involves approaching the interview with a pre-planned agenda designed to glean the data needed, avoid the pitfalls of employment law and still adapt to each manager's unique style. The interviewer must know ahead of time what he or she will ask the applicant and should stick to the agenda. Some interviewers will ask the questions in order and others will take a more relaxed approach, but they still need to address all of the pre-planned questions. This type of structure provides the interviewer with the information needed to make the hiring decision. It also ensures that no discrimination takes place.

Finally the structure establishes a solid basis for apples-to-apples comparison of the candidates.

Preparation is the key to a successful interview. In today's busy world, hiring managers or those conducting the interview are often so busy that they do not think about conducting the interview until just before the applicant arrives. If you do not prepare properly, then you end up winging it—a sure recipe for another failed hire. Planning helps you eliminate the winging-it approach and you will:

- Obtain more accurate and thorough information from each candidate.
- Be consistent with each candidate.
- Hire the right person the first time more often.
- Save a lot of money in the end.

The goals of the structured interview are:

- Promote the organization and attract the best possible candidate for the position and for the organization.
- Gather as much relevant information about the candidate as possible.
- Assess how well the candidate's overall qualifications fit all criteria for the position.
- Determine whether the candidate will fit within the organization, the culture and with the team.

The following steps are designed to assist the interviewer in preparing for and conducting the interview:

1. Review the Anti-Discrimination Guidelines prior to each interview. Avoid questions relating either directly or indirectly to age, sex, race, color, national origin, religion or disabilities. Be sure each question relates to a bona fide occupational qualification or is required by law. Refer to the guidelines on

pages 89–93 or on the accompanying CD-ROM to help you through this part of the process.

These guidelines can also be found on the accompanying CD-ROM.

2. Review each candidate's application, resume and other pre-submitted information. Note any areas needing further clarification in the interview.

3. Review your notes from the prescreening calls and the prescreening questionnaire that was submitted via an Internet job board.

4. Thoroughly familiarize yourself with the job assessment and the job description. Read it again even if you drew up the criteria yourself.

5. Before you schedule your first applicant for an interview, draw up a list of questions that will give you the information you need to make an informed decision. The outcome of your interview depends on the quality of the information you obtain from each candidate. The information received will in turn depend on the quality of your questions. Use the following resources in formulating your interview questionnaire:

    a. You will find a lengthy list of questions on the accompanying CD-ROM.

    b. You will also find the recommended Top 20 Interview Questions.

    c. If you did a personality profile during the prescreening process, you can also develop behavioral-based questions that will examine any behavioral concerns.

6. Make sure you ask all the applicants the same questions, Tailored questions may also be asked as a result of the candidate's experience, skills, education, etc.

On the accompanying CD-ROM we have included a Structured Interview Checklist that will help interviewers assess their readiness for the interviews.

STRUCTURED INTERVIEW CHECKLIST

☐ Application Reviewed
☐ Pre-Interview Questionnaire Reviewed
☐ Position Description Explained
☐ Interview Question Outline Reviewed
☐ Company Mission Statement Explained
☐ Company Ethics Policy Explained
☐ Benefit Package Explained
☐ Work Hours and Days Explained
☐ Interview Assessment Form Completed
☐ Overtime Policy Explained

☐ Background Screening, Drug Testing, and any Pre-hire testing Requirements Explained
☐ Vacation Policy Explained
☐ Trade Secret, Non-disclosure and / or (Non-compete) policy explained
☐ Substance Abuse Policy and / or Testing Explained
☐ Sexual Harassment and Discrimination Policy Explained
☐ Reference Release Explained
☐ Background Check Release Obtained

Comments: _____

Interviewer: _____ Date: _____

Structured Interview Checklist

CAUTION

Some hiring managers are using Google.com, MySpace.com, Facebook.com or other similar resources to research applicants. It is highly recommended that you NOT do this. You will most likely uncover information that is protected under various employment laws. Your knowledge and use of that information during the interview process or in employee non-selection will be considered discriminatory.

Watch Out for First Impressions

Studies have shown that the majority of hiring decisions are made within the first 10 minutes of an interview. Those decisions are based on little more than the applicant's clothing or hairstyle, a subconscious stereotype or a preconceived notion about a particular candidate or type of candidate. Indeed, the first impressions of hiring managers in initial interviews may drive the entire hiring process because they expect—and perceive—better answers from candidates who make a favorable first impression. Similarly, responses from candidates whose first impressions are disappointing can be viewed much less favorably.

As a result, many hiring managers make hiring decisions based on style rather than substance—and pass over highly qualified candidates. That's why it is so important for them to avoid presumptions. For example, the presumption that a candidate who arrives late has a tardiness problem is fundamentally flawed. Forming negative impressions about candidates who may have been caught in situations out of their control—or positive impressions about candidates because they're attractive—can be self-serving. An interview should focus on the candidate's professional experience— his or her track record of on-the-job performance.

Whether you are willing to admit it or not, you may have a predisposition that is discriminatory. Hiring today involves accepting diversity. That goes beyond the points made in the Anti-Discrimination Guidelines. You are required to set aside any prejudices against tattoos, piercings, religious symbols or ethnic attire. Hiring selections must be based on the candidate's ability to perform the tasks called for in the job description. Do not let any prejudices interfere with an honest assessment of a candidate's skills, experience and education.

Peer Interviewing

Imagine being able to handpick your co-workers. The result might be a stronger, more cohesive team that shares the company's culture. That's just one of the many benefits of peer interviewing—

a selection process that allows members of the work group to give their opinions to evaluate job candidates. Peer interviewing can provide companies with a lot of paybacks, including a higher degree of acceptance for a candidate, a higher degree of retention and a better brand recognition about your process. Peer interviewing is a critical element in building a cohesive company culture.

We recommend that peers, supervisors and even subordinates interview candidates either through a series of one-on-one interviews or as a panel. In a panel, no more than four interviewers should be present. Each is assigned one dimension on which to concentrate. For example, one person might be responsible for a skills assessment, another would interview for culture fit, and so on. Other dimensions might include programming and logic skills (for technical positions), background and past experiences, and the candidate's interest in the company and leadership skills (for management candidates). Just as you prepared for the interview, make sure your interviewers are prepared, too.

Some of these dimensions can be combined into a single interview to reduce the number of meetings. By having each interviewer focus on something different, you reduce the chance that the candidate will be asked the same questions again and again and feel compelled to give similar responses each time.

Everyone who will be interviewing must be well versed in federal and state law regulating the types of questions that may be raised in an employment interview. If you are not sure if a question violates federal or state legislation, you are better off not asking the question and checking with your legal counsel. Carefully read the following guidelines.

ANTI-DISCRIMINATION GUIDELINES

Although federal Equal Employment Opportunity (EEO) laws do not specifically prohibit any pre-employment questions, the Equal Employment Opportunity Commission does look with "extreme disfavor" on questions about age, color, disability, national origin, race, religion, gender or veteran status. Many state fair employment laws do expressly forbid certain types of questions. Following is a representative list of unacceptable and acceptable questions. It is NOT all-inclusive. We recommend you check with local resources to be sure you are in compliance with your state's laws.

Topic	Acceptable Questions	Unacceptable Questions
Age/Birth Date *Any question during the interview process that deters employment because of age is unlawful. The Age Discrimination in Employment Act of 1967 bars discrimination against persons age 40 or over.*	You can ask if the candidate is 18 years or older. If the answer is no, then you can ask the age.	"How old are you?" "What is your birth date?" "Are you a recent graduate?" "What year did you graduate?"
Arrest and Conviction Records	"Have you ever been convicted of a crime?" You can ask a candidate if he or she has had a recent conviction if it relates to the job requirement. *(Note: In most jurisdictions, this question must be accompanied by a statement on the employment application that a conviction will not necessarily disqualify applicants from the job applied for.)*	"Have you ever been arrested?" Any inquiry about convictions that are not related to job requirements.
Birthplace	"Are you legally eligible to work in the United States?"	Birthplace of the applicant, applicant's spouse, parents, or other close relatives.

ANTI-DISCRIMINATION GUIDELINES

Topic	Acceptable Questions	Unacceptable Questions
Citizenship/ National Origin	"Are you legally eligible for employment in the United States?" "Have you ever worked under a different name?"	"What is your national origin?" "Where are your parents from?" "What is your maiden name?"
Credit History or Financial Status	Credit references may be used if in compliance with the Fair Credit Reporting Act of 1970 and the Consumer Credit Reporting Reform Act of 1996.	"Do you own your own home?" "Have your wages ever been garnished?" "Have you ever declared bankruptcy?" Unless financial considerations for the job in question exist.
Disability	"Are you able to perform the duties listed in the job description you have applied for in a reasonable manner?" *(You can ask about disabilities and health after making a job offer. Then you can require a medical examination and tests for drug and alcohol use.)*	"Do you have any disabilities or handicaps?" "Have you ever been treated for a drug or alcohol problem?" "Have you had any medical problems?" Questions about general medical condition, state of health, or illness. Questions about having filed for or received workers' compensation.
Education	"Do you have a high school diploma or equivalent?" "Do you have a university or college degree?"	"When did you graduate from high school or college?"

ANTI-DISCRIMINATION GUIDELINES

Topic	Acceptable Questions	Unacceptable Questions
Emergency	"What is the name and address of the person to be notified in case of an emergency?" *(Request only after individual is employed.)*	"What is the name and address of a relative to be notified in case of an emergency?"
Marital Status *It is unlawful to deny a female applicant employment because she is pregnant or planning to have a child in the future.*	"Do you have any responsibilities or commitments that would prevent you from meeting our work schedule?"	"What is your marital status?" "Where does your spouse work?" "What are the ages of your children?" "Are you pregnant?" "Are you expecting?" "Are you married or planning to get married?"
Military Record	"What type of education, training and/or work experience did you receive while in the military?"	"When you left the military, what type of discharge did you get?" "Did you receive other than an honorable discharge from the military?"
Name	"What is your name?" "Have you ever worked for this company under a different name and if so, what was it?"	Of a married woman, "What was your maiden name?" "What is the national origin of your name?"

ANTI-DISCRIMINATION GUIDELINES

Topic	Acceptable Questions	Unacceptable Questions
Organizations	Inquiry into applicant's membership in organizations that are considered relevant to his or her ability to perform the job. "Are you a union member?"	List all clubs, societies, and lodges to which you belong.
Race or Color	There are no job-related considerations that would justify asking an applicant a question based on race. A photograph may be required for ID purposes after a hiring decision has been made.	Questions regarding complexion, color of skin, hair color or eye color. Requiring a photograph to be submitted anytime prior to hiring.
Reliability/ Punctuality and Attendance	"What hours and days can you work?" "Are there hours or days that you cannot work?" "Do you have specific responsibilities other than work that interfere with specific job requirements such as traveling?"	"How many children do you have?" "Who is going to babysit?" "Do you have pre-school-aged children at home?" "Do you have a car?"
Religion	There are no job-related considerations that would justify asking about religious conviction, unless your organization is a religious institution, which may give preference to individuals of its own religion. Statement of regular days, hours or shifts to be worked.	"Does your religion prevent you from working weekends and holidays?" "What is your religion?" "What is your church or parish?" "What religious holidays do you observe?" Applicant may not be told, "This is a Catholic [or Protestant, or Jewish, etc.] organization."

ANTI-DISCRIMINATION GUIDELINES

Topic	Acceptable Questions	Unacceptable Questions
Residence	Applicant's place of residence. "How long have you been at your present address?" "Any foreign residence?"	"Do you rent or own your home?" "How long have you lived at your present address?"
Sex (gender)	There are no appropriate questions based on gender during the interview process, except when one's gender is a bona fide occupational qualification.	A pre-employment inquiry as to sex/gender on an application form.

Here's the bottom line on effective interviewing:

- Hold the interview in a room that is private and reasonably comfortable. A conference room is best, but if you conduct the interview in your office, clear your desk, close the door and have your calls held or forwarded to voice mail. Make sure no outside interruptions occur.

- Make the applicant as comfortable as possible. This will set up a more productive dialogue. Use icebreaker questions to build rapport and set the applicant at ease. Some examples are:

  1. Did you find our office easily? How was the traffic?

  2. Would you like some coffee or water?

- Advise the applicant at the beginning of the interview session that you will be taking notes.

- Have the job description available during the interview so you can refer to it. Give a copy of the job description to the candidate so he or she can read it during the interview.

Make sure the candidate has a thorough understanding of what the position entails. Discuss how other employees have been successful in this type of position. Explain not only the duties, but your performance expectations.

- Follow your pre-planned list of questions.

- Keep an open mind when listening to answers.

- Once you have asked a question, let the applicant do the talking. Remember the 80/20 rule. You listen 80%; you talk 20%.

- Remain attentive and make sure you clearly understand the candidate's answers. If you do not, rephrase the question and ask it again.

- Observe body language, tone of voice and enthusiasm. Watch your own body language and tone.

- Jot down notes or brief responses after each question. Your notes should only contain comments from the applicant that are job-related. And remember, DO NOT write on the candidate's application form; it is a legal document that must be kept on file.

 On the accompanying CD-ROM we have provided the Interview Response Form for recording your notes and responses to the interview questions.

- Make sure that you take notes unobtrusively and do not force the candidate to pause so you can keep pace.

- Maintain control of the interview questions and time frame. If the candidate asks questions, answer them but do not lose track of your place in the interview and get engaged in an irrelevant conversation. Sales position applicants are notorious for their ability to pull you off your game plan.

- If at any time you find that the candidate is not suited for the job, courteously end the interview. It is not appropriate to waste your time or the applicant's time if it is obvious there is not a good fit.

- If you think that the applicant would be a good fit and has a solid understanding of the position and its duties, then you can engage in a little selling yourself. Give numerous reasons why your company is a good place to work.

- At the completion of the structured interview, close on a positive note. Thank all candidates for their time and let them know what the next step(s) will be (e.g., testing, reference and background checking, etc.). It is not necessary to announce a decision at this time, but it is courteous to inform the candidate what else you will be doing to evaluate his or her candidacy and when to expect a decision.

- If there are multiple interviewers, have each interviewer immediately complete a Candidate Evaluation Form on each candidate. Everyone is tired, but don't let doing this wait until tomorrow. Get the feedback right away.

On the accompanying CD-ROM we have provided a form that interviewers can use to guide their summations.

REMEMBER

The interview is just one of the essential steps in the hiring process. The results of the interview become one more measurement that must be integrated with the assessment of the resume and the application, and the results of your prescreening. In the next steps of the hiring process, you will add in testing and assessments, and reference and background checks. Do not let the results of the interview be your single source for the hiring decision. It is easy to become enamored or easily swayed by a candidate. You may be tempted to skip the rest of the hiring process because of that favorable first impression. We encourage you *not* to skip any steps in this process. You may miss that one piece of information that could have prevented hiring a "rotten egg." Trying to save a little time or money by skipping a step could result in a bad hire and cost you dearly.

On the accompanying CD-ROM you will find a lot of information to help you through this critical part of the process.

- Anti-Discrimination Guidelines
- Structured Interview Checklist
- Structured Interview Questions
- Top 20 Interview Questions
- Interview Response Form
- Candidate Evaluation Form

Candidate Evaluation Form

CANDIDATE EVALUATION FORM

Phone No.:	Date:
Name:	Reason for Interview: Initial Hire ☐ Promotion ☐
Type of Interview:	Position:
Name of Interviewer:	Job Title:
Title:	Department:
Date of Interview: Starting Date:	Name of Supervisor:
Salary:	

Criteria	Rating (1-5)	Comments
Education		
Relevant Job Experience		
Relevant Job Skills		
Supervisory Experience		
Relevant Technical Experience		
General Communication Skills Verbal Written		
General Appearance Grooming & Dress		
Knowledge of Our Company		
Enthusiasm		
Career Focus		
Special Skills		
Confidence / Demeanor		
Ambition / Motivation		
Thoroughness of Answers		
Test Scores		

Recommendation:
☐ Hire ☐ Reject ☐ Alternate Position ☐ Other: _____

Space for detailed observation on reverse side. Date: _____
Signature of Interviewer: _____

Interview Report

Observations:

STEP 7
TEST

STEP 7: TEST

In **Step 1: Define the Job** and **Step 2: Define the Person,** you took great pains to define the skill set and the personality behaviors that you felt were essential for top performance in the position. Thus far, all of your recruiting and screening has been conducted with the sole purpose of finding someone who fits the criteria that you established. Once you have completed the structured interviews, you will have identified those candidates who are truly credible and whom you believe may be able to fit the position. All of the obvious non-matches have been ruled out. Now it is time to conduct actual testing to find out if these applicants meet all of your hiring criteria. Testing will also help differentiate among all of the candidates who appear viable at this point.

It is important to understand that successful businesses are that way because they have learned to find people who can provide the diversity they need. They have learned to blend those diverse talents and personalities to fit the position, the team and the overall organizational goals and objectives.

Once Debra went on a consulting visit to a company that was struggling to grow. After conducting personality profiles of the entire organization and observing the actual operations of the company, it was easy to pinpoint why the company was having problems. The entire staff was virtually identical in their behaviors. The owner, who had conducted all of the hiring, hired people with personalities that were exactly like (or similar to) his own. The owner's personality was a "High S"—meaning he is steady, stable, structured, and likes the status quo. Consequently, dealing with change and doing things differently was out of his comfort zone.

Because hiring people who were different from him was uncomfortable for him, he basically cloned himself as he hired new employees. As a result, his hiring practices created an environment in which everyone was highly focused on getting the work accomplished. In fact, these employees were so focused that they had very little enthusiasm to solicit new customers or drive the business in a variety of ways. Hiring people who would be comfortable doing sales or working with customers proactively was a difficult concept for the owner to embrace.

When Debra told the owner that he needed to have a variety of personalities in the business to bring in enthusiasm, excitement and drive, he said he had tried that in the past, but those "types of people" tended to be disruptive. They did not mesh with his desire for a steady workforce. Since the High S personality is generally focused on production, it is a real challenge to accept others who are socially interactive and focused on sales.

This was the source of his poor business performance. His team did not contain the necessary diversity in experience and personality for optimum team performance. Once the owner understood and accepted the overall concept of building a diverse team, he was able to initiate change in his future hiring and the business soon began to blossom.

In any business, while it is important to understand the individual, success comes only when the entire team fits together and cooperates to complete the mission and achieve the vision. Teams have three challenges that they must overcome to be effective:

1. Coordination (organization based)

2. Cognition (intelligence based)

3. Cooperation (personality based)

Successfully meeting these objectives depends on establishing hiring criteria that address them precisely. That in turn dictates the need for tools that can help you evaluate each applicant against the criteria.

Coordination

Coordination depends on the existence of clear job descriptions, organization charts and well-thought-out policy and procedure manuals. It also depends on training that occurs once the applicant has actually been hired. A proper new-hire orientation builds this foundation and helps increase the coordination that is needed. It is important to understand that this only establishes the foundation; it will not be sufficient by itself if the applicant lacks the inherent capabilities to meet the other two challenges: Cognition (intelligence based) and Cooperation (personality based).

Cognitive Testing

Mathematics and Comprehension Testing

For all candidates, testing for math skills and comprehension is important. We have found the Wonderlic Personnel Test-Revised (WPT-R) to be an accurate measure of general intelligence. The WPT-R is a popular assessment tool used by employers of all kinds, even including the National Football League. This test, developed by Wonderlic, Inc. of Libertyville, Illinois, is used to determine if job applicants and football recruits have the necessary intelligence to be successful.

The WPT-R is a short (50 questions) timed (12 minutes) test that accurately measures a candidate's ability to:

- Learn a specific job.
- Solve problems.
- Understand instructions.
- Apply knowledge to new situations.
- Benefit from specific job training.
- Be satisfied with a particular job.

This test is popular because it is quick, easy to administer and delivers accurate information about the applicant's intelligence. The WPT-R enables you to match people with positions that suit their learning speed and aptitude. Through the years, Wonderlic studies have determined the minimum acceptable scores for thousands of positions in all industries. The table on the following page gives a sampling of scores drawn from the Wonderlic data.

Years ago when we formed our company, we worked with Wonderlic, Inc. to establish the criteria that would be applicable to our clients. That relationship has been extremely valuable as our company provides staffing assistance and consulting for other businesses. When we have the WPT-R results, we can feel confident when making recommendations on staffing, whether it is for hiring, promoting, training or even termination.

Equipment Testing

When the job assessment and description requires experience in the operation of specialized equipment and the applicant professes to have that ability, it is suggested that you have the candidate demonstrate his or her level of expertise. For example, this could apply to specific disciplines such as computer programming and production equipment operation. Think of it as the audition an aspiring actor would go through. Advise the candidate beforehand that such testing will be done, and allow sufficient time to accomplish it. Also be prepared to pay the candidate for the hours of actual work done.

Check with your HR department before administering tests to applicants. Keep in mind that you may also have to vary test requirements to accommodate disabled applicants. When you do administer tests, be sure they are given to all finalists for the position and that the test requirements are truly related to the position and its duties.

Minimum Acceptable Scores Wonderlic© Personnel Test-Revised

The Wonderlic Personnel Test-Revised compares the resulting score
with the minimum scores shown below for typical positions.
Over 12,000 other position minimum scores are also available.

Job Title	Minimum Acceptable Score
Accountant	28
Administrative Assistant	28
Attorney	29
Butcher	19
Customer Service Representative	24
Dental Assistant	24
Engineer	28
Event Planner	26
Executive Assistant	28
Firefighter	21
Financial Advisor	28
Information Technology Generalist	28
Investment Specialist	28
Manager	28
Marketing Specialist	26
Mechanic	17
Network Administrator	28
Nurse	26
Project Manager	26
Police Officer	22
Real Estate Agent	24
Recruiter	27
Salesperson	24
Teacher	27
Welder	22

Cooperative Testing

Cognitive testing focuses on intelligence and skills. Cooperative testing changes the focus to behavior and attitude in order to complement the specific skills testing. You will find a variety of tools that can be used to examine the behaviors and relationships of applicants. We recommend that you consider your objectives in hiring and make the selections from the available tools that will ensure the best possible hire.

Personality Profiling

In **Step 2: Define the Person**, we introduced the Thomas Personality Profiling System using the DISC methodology. Because it is so often the behavior of a person that is the ultimate reason for their termination, it is important that you make an assessment of the behavioral characteristics before you make the hire. We strongly encourage the use of a personality profile for that purpose. When our company provides staffing or consulting services, we have the candidates take a personality profile assessment as an essential and required step.

There are a variety of profiling tools available. Because of the ease of use and the clarity of the results, we have always relied on profiles using the DISC method. Please refer back to the discussion in **Step 2: Define the Person** to better understand this methodology.

As mentioned throughout this book, we support the use of the Thomas Personality Profiling System. This system is based on the DISC methodology and is validated, reliable, and accessible online. It also works well within the overall intention of the U.S. Equal Employment Opportunity Commission (EEOC) guidelines and the Canadian Human Rights Act.

The Thomas Personality Profiling System is a powerful workplace inventory and can be used in virtually every aspect of human relations within the work environment. The assessment tool for the Thomas System is a simple questionnaire, available in hard copy or online, that presents 24 groups of words or phrases. Each group contains four background descriptive terms from which the candidate selects the one most like and the one least like them. The simplicity of the questionnaire belies the complexity of the results. The basic report generated from the assessment is the Personal Profile Analysis (PPA). The PPA provides an overview of an individual's basic behavioral characteristics, self-image, primary motivators, recommended job emphasis, behavior modification in the work environment, and predicted behavior under pressure. This in-depth assessment is suitable for hiring and coaching individuals. It is the foundation report recommended for anyone interested in a detailed analysis on an employee, candidate, or co-worker, as well as those interested in exploring self-analysis.

On the accompanying CD-ROM you will find a sample report.

A significant feature of the PPA is its analysis of the reaction of the individual under stress. In many businesses, managers and employees often operate under stress. Whether it is customer demands, financial concerns, employee issues or even the weather, the result is a stressful environment. For that reason, it is clearly beneficial to understand how stress affects the behavior of an applicant before you make a hiring decision.

Once the assessment is completed, additional reports can be generated for greater understanding of relationships necessary for building a strong team. The system also has the ability to evaluate the personality in terms of certain key positions. Reports can be generated that evaluate applicants against specific criteria for management, sales and customer service roles.

When preparing for the structured interview, the system can generate unique behavioral-based interview questions that facilitate the investigation of any areas of concern. These questions are used during the structured interview to more completely understand the applicant. These questions can also be used in the reference-checking process to shape specific, direct questions that help find out how the applicant behaved in earlier employments. See the table below for a list of the additional reports, position audits and interviewing aids that can be generated from this system.

Additional Thomas Profile Reports

Call Center Audit	This report is specifically designed to assess an individual in relation to a call center environment. It reports on handling peak workloads, handling aggressive clients and meeting client needs. Indicates suitability for inbound and outbound environments.
Candidate Feedback	If you only require a brief one-page analysis that you intend to provide to a prospective candidate, this is an ideal cost-effective choice. This is a brief summary report, user friendly and very positive, which summarizes the individual's behavioral style and reports on the likely value he or she will bring to the organization. A simple, effective report to create self-awareness and to develop individuals.
Career Guide	This guide provides a summary of people's key behaviors, motivation and job emphasis and then lists specific functions and job types that are best suited to their characteristics and the occupation level selected. For the person considering a new career opportunity, or if you are new to the job market, this is a useful guide. When considering reassignment or reorganization with the company, this guideline will help define the strengths this person will bring to other positions. Career Guidelines can be used in succession planning and career guidance coaching. Three "levels" are available for clerical/manual, supervisor/middle management and executive/senior management functions.
Comparison	This report compares the individual's profile to the behavioral job requirements established in the Human Job Analysis in Step 2 and identifies the "goodness of fit."
Compatibility	This report assesses the compatibility of two people. It can be used to enhance the way people work together and it helps create a respect for differences and leveraging strengths optimally.

Additional Thomas Profile Reports

Customer Service Audit	The report provides an analysis of ability to understand client needs, handle aggression and criticism, and respond to client requests. It also looks at presentation and communication skills, creativity, problem solving and possible limitations in serving clients. Overall customer service skills are rated in three distinct service categories. It may also be used to enhance customer service skills in sales people.
Executive Summary	This report is for the busy manager or recruiter who is familiar with the Thomas DISC system. It is designed to highlight the essential elements of an individual's behavior profile. The content is concise and to the point.
General Interview Questionnaire	This report produces a generic set of interview questions in conjunction with a review of the candidate's profile. It is designed for use in any role, and the questions help probe the candidate's abilities to modify natural behaviors to be successful in the role.
How to Effectively Manage	This report is a blueprint for managing that new person optimally and can often speed up the integration time of that employee into the company and team, and build a better manager/employee relationship fast.
Management Audit	This report provides an analysis of management and motivational skills, decision-making style, approach to planning and problem solving, communication skills, subordinate development and administrative abilities. It also identifies specific management skills and/or training requirements of new and existing managers and potential management candidates from outside or within the organization.
Management Interview Questionnaire	This is a detailed series of questions designed for use in identifying management capability in a candidate. Each report is automatically customized to the person you are assessing and it is recommended that this format be used in the initial interview.
Sales Audit	This analysis will provide a critique of a person's selling style in six different areas that include closing and customer service. This summary is very useful when selecting, developing, or coaching sales staff or in determining one's own strengths and weaknesses in sales.
Sales Interview Questionnaire	Specifically geared to focus the interview with sales professionals, this questionnaire provides a framework to help you determine if a person has what it takes to sell your product or service. The report will also provide an opinion on a person's sales compatibility.

Additional Thomas Profile Reports

Strengths and Limitations Summary	This report summarizes people's positive behavioral traits as well as the value they can contribute to an organization. It also includes a description of the possible challenges or shortcomings of his or her style. This is very useful summary when used in the context of comparing oneself to a job requirement or specific role.
Technical/ Administrative Audit	For those in a technical or administrative role, this report is designed to explore how people function in areas such as organizing workflow, meeting deadlines, problem solving and ensuring quality.
Training Needs Analysis	This report starts with a brief description of the person's most pronounced strengths and limitations. It goes on to identify likely training needs and details competencies and challenges in relation to those needs. It also provides suggestions as to what training could be given to develop greater ability to flex behaviors and increase success.

We especially recommend that you obtain the Comparison Report described in the table above because it clearly evaluates the applicant against the HJA and defines the "goodness of fit." Through Debra's training with Dr. Tom Hendrickson, who pioneered this profile analysis methodology, we learned to understand how the various characteristics work together. We are now able to evaluate the fit with the position and the rest of the team. We personally find great satisfaction in using the profile to help team members understand each other as internal customers and build productivity by emphasizing the importance of satisfying that type of customer.

Emotional Intelligence Testing

It is minimally essential that the hiring managers look at both the WPT-R and the personality profile results before making a hiring decision. However, in some cases it may be necessary to expand the testing to look at other traits or emotions that the applicant brings to the position. This is particularly true in managerial positions where an ability to understand and relate to the staff is vital. We often recommend an additional assessment that examines the candidate's overall emotional intelligence. This is a measure of the individual's ability to adapt to the environment as well as to survive and thrive. To give some understanding of this concept, let's consider an area we have already evaluated for the applicant.

The WPT-R was a simple test to evaluate the Intelligence Quotient (IQ). IQ is a measure of our intellectual, analytical, logical and rational abilities. It gauges how readily we learn new things; how we focus on tasks and exercises; how we retain and recall objective information; how we engage in the reasoning process and manipulate numbers; how we think abstractly as well as analytically; and how we solve problems by applying prior knowledge.

We all know people who may be quite (cognitive) intelligent, but can't make good in either their personal or working lives. They rub others the wrong way; success just doesn't seem to pan out. Much of the time, they can't figure out why. The main reason is they are deficient in certain aspects of emotional intelligence. Studies have shown that IQ can only serve to predict an average of 6% of success in a given job based on Richard Wagner's 1997 meta-analysis. Emotional intelligence, on the other hand, has been found to be directly responsible for 27% to 45% of job success. One of the most prolific researchers and practitioners in this area, Reuven Bar-On has found that the correlation between emotional intelligence and occupational performance is .55 (which is high) based on six major studies that examined 3,500 individuals worldwide. The book *The Millionaire Mind* by Thomas Stanley is based on a survey of 733 multimillionaires throughout the United States. They rated the following factors as the top five responsible for their success:

- Being honest with people
- Being well disciplined
- Getting along with people
- Having a supportive spouse
- Working harder than most people

These factors are directly or indirectly associated with emotional intelligence. The measure of emotional intelligence is called the "Emotional Quotient" (EQ), which was coined by Reuven Bar-On.

In creating his instrument for evaluating the Emotional Quotient, Bar-On called it "an array of non-cognitive capabilities, competencies and skills that influence one's ability to succeed in coping with environmental demands and pressures." Additionally, these very important human attributes are a comprehensive assortment of emotional and social factors that impact successful behavior as well. Peter Salovey and Jack Mayer describe "emotional intelligence" as "the ability to perceive emotions, to access and generate emotions so as to assist thought, to understand emotions and emotional meanings, and to reflectively regulate emotions in ways that promote emotional and intellectual growth."

Emotional intelligence is what we commonly refer to as "street smarts" or "common sense." It has to do with the ability to emotionally read oneself and others; to intuitively grasp what others want and need, what their strengths and weaknesses are; to remain unruffled by stress; and to be engaging—the kind of person that others want to be around.

Our personalities and our IQ remain relatively unchanged over time. Like IQ, the traits that comprise our personalities are fixed from about 18 years of age. If we are inclined to be honest, introverted or loyal, it's highly unlikely we would strike off in a new and unexpected direction. Psychologists call these traits "static," and term an individual's personality as a whole "strategic"— another way of saying that it operates over the long haul. Emotional intelligence, however, is made up of flexible, tactical, and "dynamic" competencies and skills that can be brought into play as the situation warrants. EQ can also be improved through training, coaching and experience, which is extremely difficult if not impossible to do with IQ.

In developing his instrument for evaluating EQ, Bar-On divided emotional intelligence into the following five key areas and 15 subfactors:

1. **Intrapersonal Capacity** concerns your ability to know, understand and manage yourself.

   a. Self-awareness: the ability to recognize how you are feeling and why you are feeling that way and the impact your behavior has on others.

   b. Assertiveness: the ability to clearly express your thoughts and feelings, stand your ground and defend a position.

   c. Independence: the ability to be self-directed and self-controlled, to stand on your own two feet.

   d. Self-regard: the ability to accurately recognize your strengths and weaknesses and to feel good about yourself despite your weaknesses.

   e. Self-actualization: the ability to realize your potential, set and pursue personal goals, and to feel comfortable with what you achieve at work and in your personal life.

2. **Interpersonal Capacity** concerns your people skills—that is, your ability to understand people and to interact and get along with others.

   a. Empathy: the ability to understand what others might be feeling and thinking. It is the ability to view the world through another person's eyes.

   b. Social responsibility: the ability to be a cooperative and contributing member of your social group.

   c. Interpersonal relationship: the ability to forge and maintain relationships that are mutually beneficial and marked by give-and-take and a sense of emotional closeness.

3. **Adaptability** involves your ability to be flexible and realistic and to solve personal and interpersonal problems as they arise.

a. Reality testing: the ability to see things as they actually are, rather than the way you wish or fear they might be.

b. Flexibility: the ability to adjust your feelings, thoughts and actions to changing conditions.

c. Problem-solving: the ability to define personal and interpersonal problems and then generate and implement realistic, appropriate and effective solutions.

4. **Stress Management** concerns your ability to manage stress and control impulses.

a. Stress tolerance: the ability to remain calm and focused, to constructively withstand adverse events and conflicting emotions without caving in.

b. Impulse control: the ability to resist or delay a temptation to act.

5. **General Mood**

a. Optimism: the ability to maintain a realistically positive attitude, particularly in the face of adversity.

b. Happiness: the ability to feel satisfied with life, to enjoy yourself and others, and to experience zest and enthusiasm in a range of activities.

Regardless of how brainy we may be, if we turn others off with abrasive behavior, are unaware of how we are presenting ourselves or cave in under minimal stress, no one will stick around long enough to notice our high IQ's.

Bar-On Emotional Quotient-Inventory (EQ-i®)

The Bar-On EQ-i® is based on the most comprehensive theory of emotional intelligence to date and is used in hiring, succession planning and personnel development. The Bar-On EQ-i® consists of 133 questions, which, when responded to, quantify the five key components and 15 subfactors of emotional intelligence. The completion of this instrument takes approximately 30 minutes and produces a multipage report that includes the scale scores and explains what they mean as well as provides suggestions for strengthening the weaker aspects of the individual's emotional intelligence. The report explains what these quantified results mean as far as the individual's current performance is concerned.

While it is important to understand our applicants' levels of emotional intelligence, the value of the EQ-i® is not just in providing test results, but in the assistance that it can bring to a constructive mentoring and coaching effort as well as in hiring and succession. Proper use of this information drawn from the EQ-i® can help individuals develop their ability to relate successfully to others in the work environment and increase occupational performance and overall organizational productivity. It is important to understand that emotional intelligence can always be further developed and improved upon.

Bottom Line

Failing to test candidates is one of the biggest mistakes that employers make in hiring. Too often they need "a body" so desperately that they rely on their gut instincts to make a selection rather than taking advantage of the many tools available to help make a more informed decision.

The tests described in this step help bring objectivity to the hiring process that interviews alone cannot do. It is absolutely essential that you evaluate intelligence and personality as part of the selection process. It is too expensive to bring in new employees and then find out later that they do not have the smarts to learn the job or they do not fit the culture of the company or the rest of the team. Hiring requires due diligence to find out everything that you can to make a correct hiring decision. These assessment tools are absolutely necessary and should never be neglected in the process.

Many hiring managers are concerned with what they can or cannot do within the guidelines of the EEOC. The tools we are recommending are all fully validated and compliant with the provisions of the EEOC. Whether you use the tools that we like or find other comparable tools, verify that they are validated and that they are EEOC compliant. If you do, you can be comfortable in their use and confident in their results.

Getting It Done

Larger companies are in a position to work with the assessment agencies and make arrangements to get the instruments they need as well as the counseling needed to properly utilize the results. It is more of a challenge for small businesses to gain access to these instruments because of the smaller volume of testing they would do. A large part of our business is assisting small businesses to overcome this challenge. We strongly urge the use of these tools and encourage you to contact us. Our assistance will make it possible for you to hire Grade AA talent.

On the accompanying CD-ROM you will find samples of all of the reports from the Thomas Personality Profiling System and a sample of the emotional intelligence report.

STEP 8: REFERENCE CHECK

Reference checking is an important, but often frustrating, aspect of the hiring process. When done well, the reference checking process helps hiring managers screen "in" qualified candidates who are good fits for the job and the organization and screen "out" unsuitable individuals. Checking references is another tool to help you hire the right person the first time. DO NOT eliminate this step just because the candidate "appears" good. A few phone calls can verify the information you have received through applications, resumes and interviews. The reference check confirms if the candidate's past performance measures up to the criteria you have established for the position.

A critical step hiring managers should take is preventative action to reduce the threat of workplace violence and losses due to theft. Reference checking enables hiring managers to determine if applicants have any history of violence or dishonesty. Moreover, obtaining information about applicants' past job performances and work habits enables employers to identify and reject individuals who are incompetent or have a history of discipline problems or chronic absenteeism. By avoiding the "rotten eggs" who would be a poor fit, you will reap rewards in increased productivity and reduced turnover with the right hires.

It is true that employers face challenges both in getting and giving references, but effective processes can provide distinct advantages. Here are three key employer objectives in obtaining references:

1. **Verify information**: In an ideal world, reference checking would be unnecessary because employers could rely on all statements made by applicants in resumes, employment applications and interviews. In the real world, employers proceed at their peril if they fail to verify what applicants

tell them. The magnitude of deception that occurs during the hiring process is staggering. Numerous studies report that 25% to 40% of applicants provide false, exaggerated, or misleading information about their qualifications or backgrounds. One survey by Reid Psychological Systems even found that the college students polled said they would lie to get a job and 41% of them had already done so.

2. **Protect the organization and its employees:** Sound reference checking practices can help organizations avoid two serious problems plaguing workplaces throughout the United States: workplace violence and employee theft.

3. **Avoid legal problems associated with poor hiring decisions:** Employers run the risk of lawsuits for negligent hiring if they fail to exercise reasonable care in investigating an applicant's background and hire an unsuitable individual who harms others in a way that was foreseeable based on that person's background. These lawsuits can be quite costly. The average settlement in lawsuits for negligent hiring exceeds $1.6 million, according to American Background Information Services, Inc.

Meeting these three objectives will enable an employer to hire the best candidates, avoid hiring disasters, reduce costs, and increase productivity.

When the applicant completed the application form, he or she signed a release to check references. It is important to have the applicant's permission to conduct the checking to avoid any claim for invasion of privacy by the applicant. You do not have to have a signed release as long as you have informed the candidate verbally that you would be checking references and the candidate did not object. Also, if the candidate provides you with references, this is tacit agreement that you have permission to contact his or her references.

Please note the courtesy that must be extended to an applicant who is currently employed. Checking references with the current employer could jeopardize the applicant's standing. Those references should be checked, but do not do it until after the applicant has accepted your offer. The offer becomes contingent on the reference checking results and any other checks that are completed.

In most cases, reference checking can be done by telephone, but sometimes it may require written communication. This may be necessary if the company given as a reference has a policy of only responding in writing. You may also prefer to do it this way for key management positions or before agreeing to significantly higher salaries. In those cases, a letter to the former employer on your company letterhead along with the Request for Verification of Employment with a signed authorization from the candidate may be more appropriate than a phone call.

In looking at references of someone who has been in the workforce, we recommend you focus on the professional references and not be sidetracked by glowing personal references. If the only references are from friends and family, it is highly unlikely that you will get a true picture of the person in a work environment—unless the family/friends are also involved in the business the candidate is referencing. (This, of course, is different for young people just entering the workforce because they have not had the opportunity to demonstrate any work experience.)

We so often hear employers objecting to the idea of doing reference checking because they maintain they will not learn anything. The truth could not be more different. When we conduct reference checks for businesses, we are almost always able to get meaningful and valuable information from former employers. Even if a reference will only verify dates of employment, position title, and starting and ending salary, this information can sometimes be priceless.

You may learn that basic information provided by the candidate is not the same as that obtained from the reference. If this occurs, it should raise a huge red flag—one that should make you get further clarification from the candidate or get more information before proceeding any further with this candidate.

We have found that if we are well prepared to make the reference call, we will get all the information we need, plus more. To get prepared we:

1. Fill in the information we have about the candidate on our Telephone Reference Checking form.

2. Review the results of the personality profile and have a few specific questions directly relating to the individual's profile. Often, the results of a profile might indicate that people are not "user-friendly" under stress, or that they lack the detail orientation you are requiring, or that they are a highly social/outgoing person who wastes time rather than the steady, stable, quiet type. When conducting your reference checks, this is the perfect opportunity to ask pointed questions about any of these concerns you may have. The reference is usually so surprised that you already have specific questions, they are very willing to elaborate about your concerns.

3. After placing the reference call and connecting with the right person, introduce yourself saying who gave you his or her name and number. Next, ask if this is a good time to ask a few questions and, if not, schedule a time to reconnect that is convenient. Let the person know that the conversation will not take long, but it is important for you to get as much information as possible because your intent is to set up a win-win situation. Inform the reference that you do not want to hire a person who will not fit into your culture or the open position and ultimately not be happy at your place of business.

4. If the reference is unwilling to answer questions beyond the basics, the most telling question you can ask is, "Would you ever consider rehiring this candidate?" If there is "dead air" at the other end of the phone, you have your answer.

5. Always end your conversations by thanking all references for their time. If appropriate, let them know you will inform the candidate that they took the time to provide the necessary information.

If you cannot reach a reference right away, leave a message indicating your request to conduct a reference interview on a particular person and it will only take a few minutes of their time. However, always be sensitive when leaving a message because it may not be appropriate to share the candidate's name with this particular person.

In making a hire, it is important the information indicates a consistent pattern. The following are not necessarily disqualifiers but they do indicate the need for further checking:

- No references provided or unable to locate named references
- No direct supervisors listed as references
- All previous companies are "out of business"
- References at previous companies have left the company
- Previous income inconsistent with responsibilities or title
- Only home numbers provided for references
- Applicant has negative comments about references
- Reason for termination is vague
- Reference responses and information are evasive or vague
- Reference responses are overly complimentary

The accompanying CD-ROM contains sample forms to help in the reference-checking process. The Reference Checking Form is intended for use while conducting each telephone reference check. The Request for Verification of Employment Form is intended for use when written communication is needed to obtain information. This form is formatted to be reproduced on your letterhead.

Reference Checking
Form

STEP 9
HIRING
DECISION

STEP 9: HIRING DECISION

This step of the hiring process helps you identify the best candidate from your finalists. Decision-makers in companies with good track records for successful hiring do not trust their intuition alone. Instead, they use a system that provides an objective comparison and evaluation of all of the information they have gathered. While many times only one candidate clearly stands out from the pack, occasionally multiple candidates have many of the capabilities defined in the job assessment and description. While all of the candidates at this point possess the desired job requirements to a sufficient degree, it is likely there are still variations in the way each candidate meets the criteria. A structured evaluation is the key to obtaining an "apples-to-apples" comparison.

We cannot emphasize enough that you should only make a hiring decision from among acceptable candidates. During the hiring at several junctures, emerging results can identify candidates who have failed to meet the minimum acceptable levels for your criteria. They should have been dropped from consideration as soon as their weakness was evident. The process of evaluating candidates is like a funnel with only suitable candidates emerging from it. At this point when you are trying to decide among your best candidates, make sure they all meet your criteria. The hiring process should quantitatively identify the one who best meets those criteria.

If you are fortunate to have more than one qualified candidate, create a matrix based on the criteria you established for the position. Weight each criterion in accordance with its importance to the position and its requirements. Establish the criteria and the weighting before you begin to score the candidates. Otherwise you might be tempted to weight the criteria to fit one of the candidates and not your position requirements. The set of values you assign to the weighting is not the main consideration. Whether everything is spread across a scale of 100 or a scale of 1,000, the important factor is that the criteria are properly weighted relative to each other. Is education more important than experience? Are aptitude and attitude more important than skill level? Which of your skill requirements is most important? Assign the weighting that accurately defines the importance of each of the criteria.

Then develop a rating system that rates each candidate against the criteria. That could be a scale of one to four like this: one = does not meet; two = meets; three = exceeds; four = far exceeds the requirement. Include in the rating process all staff members who participated in the interviewing process. It may be necessary to have each interviewer complete the matrix independently to avoid peer pressure. If that results in a difference of opinion on who is the best candidate, then discuss each of the assessments to see if certain issues noted by one interviewer were not caught by the others.

While the criteria must be specific to the position that you are filling, the chart on the following page represents a sample decision matrix:

Sample Decision Matrix
Position: Customer Service Representative

Criterion	Requirement	Weight	Candidate 1		Candidate 2	
			Rating	Score	Rating	Score
Experience						
Customer Service	3-5 years	10	3	30	4	40
Industry Specific	3-5 years	5	4	20	4	20
Computer/ Software Skills	PC, Office, ACT!	8	2	16	3	24
Communication Skills	Excellent	10	3	30	4	40
Education	BA or Equivalent	4	4	16	2	8
Wonderlic©	> 24	10	3	30	4	40
Personality / HJA Comparison	Goodness of fit > 3	10	3	30	2	20
	> 120	10	4	40	3	30
Salary Desired	<$12 per hr	5	4	20	3	15
Work Schedule	FT and OT	8	4	32	4	32
Interview	Positive	10	3	30	4	40
References	Positive	10	3	30	3	30
		Total Score		324		339

In this example, Candidate 1 scored 324 and Candidate 2 scored 339. Both of them scored very well, but the nod goes to Candidate 2. The logical approach is to now move forward to Step 10 and make an offer to Candidate 2. Often, a candidate will get this far in the hiring process, but when the offer is made, the deal falls apart. Candidate 1 then becomes your backup if you are unable to reach an employment agreement with your first choice.

If you have truly objectively evaluated all of the criteria and the candidates' ability to meet them, then the numerical assessment should indicate the best candidate. If you have two candidates who score exactly the same, we recommend you bring them back for additional interviews, particularly if the original interviewers had disagreed on some matters. Then reevaluate the candidates to see if the scoring changed. Don't change your criteria or their weighting; just determine if the candidate rating is correct.

Bad hiring decisions result from a failure to do something you should have done. Whatever happens, do not deviate from the initial requirements (Job Description and Human Job Analysis) that you established in the beginning. Those criteria were what you defined for the job and for the person. Resist the temptation to hire someone just because you need to fill the job. A hasty hire will result in a hiring mistake that will cost you money and more time. Also avoid the halo effect. The term "halo effect" refers to the tendency to focus on how much you liked the candidate's appearance or how much you have in common with the person rather than how well the candidate fits the requirements of the job. The selection process is designed to aid the well-seasoned judgment of the hiring manager, not replace this judgment. In the end every hiring decision is a judgment call, but if you use the tools provided in this hiring process to help you make an informed decision, you will be better off.

While we recommend against hurried hiring decisions, it is highly recommended that each decision be made in a timely manner. Often, for very critical positions, there are only a few suitable candidates—and remember that your competitors are seeking the same talent. Too many times, the hiring manager hesitates awhile before proceeding with the offer—only to find the applicant has accepted another position. This is particularly true when the candidate is the top performer you really want. The hiring process cannot be hasty, but all of the steps should be completed at a steady pace without long delays.

If only one applicant has met all of the criteria and you are sure you made an objective assessment, do not avoid making the hiring decision in hopes another applicant will show up. Remember the old adage, "A bird in hand is worth two in the bush." When conducting the hiring process for companies that we work with, we often submit qualified candidates to hiring managers and hear them respond, "This person looks good and we really like her, but do you have someone else we can compare her to?" However, in today's job market, we see fewer applicants for positions and an even fewer yet who can meet reasonable hiring criteria.

No doubt it is not easy to reach a decision to hire, but if you have gone through the process and the applicant meets all the criteria for skills, education, intelligence, and personality, make an offer without delay to bring that person on board immediately.

On the accompanying CD-ROM you will find a Decision Matrix Form and a sample of a completed Decision Matrix.

STEP 10: MAKE OFFER

You have reached a critical phase in the hiring of Grade AA talent. You have invested a lot of time, energy and money into the process of recruiting and selecting the right person for your open position. After evaluating all of the qualified candidates, you have identified the one who best meets your criteria. Now it is time to move quickly since good candidates may disappear. Making an offer is crucial to the creation of a long-term relationship with this candidate. Conveying the offer in a timely fashion is important, but it is just as important to make sure that you are clear on what you are offering. Whether it is stated in the verbal or the written offer, the terms of the employment must be made clear and any conditions yet to be satisfied must also be made clear. Successful organizations realize that these initial steps in making the candidate an employee will form a bond that can influence how long this top performer stays with your company.

We recommend that you make a verbal offer as soon as you are sure of your hiring decision and have established all of the elements of the compensation and benefits package. Communicate that information to the candidate and inform him or her that you will be following up with a formal written offer.

Remember that the position comes with conditions for both the hiring manager and the new employee. The offer is key to making sure all those conditions and agreements are understood by both you and the candidate. The offer letter in particular puts in writing all the terms of the job offer in order to preclude any misunderstanding. It becomes a binding agreement on both parties so make sure it is clear and fully understood. If questions arise from the candidate, discuss them fully and revise the offer letter so that all ambiguities are cleared up.

The offer letter usually represents the first written communication with your prospective new employee. Therefore, it should reflect your enthusiasm and make the new employee feel welcome. It should also recognize that the candidate has passed your difficult standards and he or she should be congratulated for that achievement. Think over all that you have learned about your candidate and then see what you can incorporate into the written offer of employment that will entice him or her to join your organization.

Compensation is, of course, a major part of the offer. Therefore make sure you know what the market is paying for the particular position. Professional organizations often publish salary surveys that provide a good starting point. Also, you can research websites such as Salary.com, Payscale.com, and the U.S. Bureau of Labor Statistics Wages, Earnings and Benefits section at BLS.gov. Compensation must be commensurate with the experience and education of the candidate and competitive with offers from other employers. As you look at the salary statistics for your industry, also remember that "average wages are for average employees."

Offer letters that spell out the major terms and conditions of the employment relations are vital to setting clear expectations between the company and employee. Therefore, include as many details as practical in your job offer letter along with attachments or enclosures so your candidate has enough information to make an informed decision. Remember, candidates might receive other job offers so you are competing for their attention.

Here is a list of subjects that should be covered in the letter:

- The job title and the supervisor to whom he or she will report.
- Scope of the responsibilities and duties drawn from the job description. (You should attach the job description.)
- The expected start date.

- Compensation spelled out in annual salary or hourly rates and the frequency of payment (weekly, bi-weekly, monthly). If there are incentives associated with the position, they should also be clearly defined.

- Benefits package and appropriate disclosure information on health benefits and exclusions.

- Information on confidentiality and protection of trade secrets agreements.

- Additional requirements that still must be met such as proof of citizenship, Social Security card, diplomas, etc.

- The offer is made contingent on satisfactory completion of additional conditions such as a drug test or a physical examination, security clearance, additional reference checks (if necessary) and a background check.

- A release letter for the background check, if not already obtained.

- If the position requires an employment contract or a non-compete agreement, include it for the employee to read and approve.

- Relocation arrangements or any other special agreements you have made with the candidate.

- If the company is an "at-will" employer, that should be specified as well.

- A deadline for acceptance of the offer.

Make sure you do not:

- Promise raises, bonuses, vacations or perks that may not be forthcoming.

- Make any guarantees that the employee will be employed for any length of time.

- Promise anything that you cannot provide.

Once you have written the offer letter, then contact the applicant and make the offer verbally using the offer letter as a guide to the conversation. This gives you a chance to openly communicate your enthusiasm and, of course, evaluate the candidate's response and reactions. Whether the candidate accepts or not, send the offer letter immediately. Once it is read, there may be conditions that the candidate, in his or her eagerness to accept, did not fully understand. There may still be other hurdles to overcome. On the other hand, the offer letter could clarify points that the applicant didn't understand and he or she might have a change of heart and decide to accept the offer. While you may proceed with making the written offer, we highly recommend you remind the candidate that he or she could be terminated or released from further employment depending on the results of the background investigation or any other requirements still pending.

As soon as an offer letter is sent, follow up immediately with the candidate to ensure it includes everything he or she expected. Being proactive may help facilitate an offer's acceptance and also convey a positive message to the candidate. If you are going to attract the very best talent, you have to do what it takes to sell the organization to those desired candidates.

Even after acceptance, remember that the candidate is still only a potential employee until he or she reports for work and fills out all of the paperwork as a new employee. It has been known to happen that the distance between acceptance and the start date turns into infinity. We can cite far too many instances when candidates accepted and then changed their minds. Sometimes, their current company makes a counteroffer they cannot refuse or they are just overcome with the fear of something new.

Be prepared that your offer may be rejected. It is always possible that the applicant may turn you down. After all, the interview process was also his or her way to evaluate taking the job. There are two options when that occurs. First, if your job assessment indicated that some areas of the position were negotiable and these were the basis for the candidate's refusal, then it might be acceptable to amend the offer. But if your budget for the position was set, do not make wage offers you cannot afford, and most important, don't minimize your requirements for the position. If you do agree to certain changes, put those into a new offer letter to make sure that everyone is on the same page. Do not allow verbal changes to go unrecorded.

The second option is to go back to your list of acceptable candidates and make the offer to the next ACCEPTABLE candidate. If there were no other acceptable candidates, it is necessary to go back to **Step 3: Recruit.** As painful as it may be after getting this far in the process, you will be better off starting all over again.

On the accompanying CD-ROM you will find a format for a sample offer letter.

Sample Offer Letter

Step 10: Make Offer

STEP 11
FINAL
CHECKS

STEP 11: FINAL CHECKS

The process for hiring Grade AA talent often feels like a long and difficult journey. But now you are nearing the end. You have selected a winner, and your offer has been accepted. You are ready to get back to work and be done with this hiring distraction. But before you start the victory celebration for bringing on this winner, you still need to complete several actions. Remember, your offer letter included a number of contingencies that needed to be satisfied before your candidate can become an official employee.

In **Step 8: Reference Check**, you initiated reference checking to validate information the candidate provided about his or her previous work experience. Make sure you complete all of those calls. The references may still disclose information that could cause you to reconsider your offer. Still other checks will be dictated by company or insurance policies and the need to avoid the potential for a negligent hire. The nature of your business could also require obtaining a security clearance.

Drug Testing

We highly recommend that organizations have a policy in place to deal with substance abuse. Drug testing is becoming commonplace for many large companies and even some high schools. But substance abuse may be an even greater concern for the small business owner. According to OSHA, "When it comes to workplace substance abuse, small businesses have big disadvantages. They are less likely than large companies to have programs in place to combat the problem, yet they are more likely to be the 'employer-of-choice' for illicit drug users. Individuals who cannot adhere to a drug-free workplace policy seek employment at firms that do not have one, and the cost of just one accident caused by an impaired employee can devastate a small business."

Additional statistics to consider:

- 65% of accidents on the job are caused by substance abuse (OSHA): Employees who abuse drugs file six times more workers' compensation claims than those who don't. (*Occupational Health & Safety Magazine*)

- Health benefit utilization of employees that use drugs is 84% greater in dollar terms. These employees record 16 times more work absences. (U.S. Dept. of Labor)

- The vast majority of drug users are employed. When they arrive for work, they don't leave their problems at the door. Of the 16.7 million illicit drug users aged 18 or older in 2003, 12.4 million (74.3%) were employed either full or part-time. Furthermore, research indicates that between 10% and 20% of the nation's workers who die on the job test positive for alcohol or other drugs. (OSHA)

You must be prepared to deal with this issue. If you do not already have a policy on substance abuse, you should begin immediately to create a detailed policy and procedure. To help small businesses benefit from being drug-free, the Department of Labor and OSHA's Working Partners for an Alcohol- and Drug-Free Workplace program offers small businesses a range of free and easy-to-use tools to help them maintain safe, healthy and drug-free workplaces. For more information, go to osha.gov and select Safety/Health issues. Tools available are:

- Drug-Free Workplace Advisor Program Builder—information employers need to develop a drug-free workplace policy from scratch

- Substance Abuse Information Database (SAID)—online repository of hundreds of documents related to workplace drug abuse, including sample policies, surveys, research reports, training and educational materials, and legal and regulatory information

- Resource Directories—regularly updated lists of national, state and local resources, including summaries of state laws related to workplace substance abuse, community-based organizations that assist in making businesses drug-free, and help-lines that offer assistance to individuals who have, or know someone who has, a drug problem

- Training and Educational Materials—resources such as presentation materials, articles and fact sheets, and posters to help employers provide drug and alcohol education in the workplace

Background Checking

Statistics reveal that nearly 40% of employment application information from applicants is falsified. More statistics from 2005 Annual Applicant Statistics as reported by InfoLink Screening Services include:

- 8.5% have a criminal record.
- 41.0% have motor vehicle violations including DUIs and possession of drugs.
- 41.2% of credit reports include negative information.
- 36.5% of past employment verifications had inconsistencies.
- 14.1% provided false or inconsistent information about their education.
- 8.5% provided false or inconsistent information about professional license certifications.
- 25.2% provided false or inconsistent military service information.

Therefore, your next action is to proceed with background checking. Background reports normally include a person's criminal history, arrest warrants/felony convictions and driving record, as well as credit information. This kind of "undercover" work is now standard in many small businesses largely due to the potential liability for negligent hiring. You are responsible to your employees, your customers and yourself to know ahead of time who you are hiring. The hiring process is an exercise in completing due diligence. Your reference checking should have disclosed any serious problems, but if it did not fully disclose everything, the background check should.

Remember, the applicant and/or employee must grant authorization to complete the background investigation. A separate release form will be needed and should be included in your offer letter. To help you through this, we highly recommend you contact a background investigation agency to assist in the process. The agency's system should provide you with authorization forms, Fair Credit Reporting compliance, and likely "immunity from civil action" by using its service. The data needed to conduct the background check includes the candidate's Social Security number, birth date, driver's license information, and current and previous addresses. Because of concerns over identity theft associated with the information that is needed, it is essential that the candidate signs the release form.

Most background checking agencies/resources use computer programs and public information to provide concise, easy-to-read reports outlining the applicant's past history, felony convictions within the last seven years and a credit report. They also have the capability of examining, verifying or validating any information claimed on a job application that may be critical to the hiring decision. They also have the capability (at added cost) of verifying work experience and education.

Here is a list of information that can be made available to you. Some agencies offer a package that includes two to four of the reports listed below:

- Criminal History (local and out-of-state)

- Previous Employers

- Social Security Verification

- Education

- Motor Vehicle Driving Records

- Professional License

- Public Records

- Military Service Verification

- Credit History

- Arrest Warrants/Felony Conviction

You can find security companies and private investigators in the Yellow Pages under "Personnel Services" or "Employment Screening." Routine checks can start as low as $50 depending on where you live, how much information you request and the prior mobility of your new employee.

You can also check online for companies that offer background-checking services. A simple keyword search of "background checks" on the major search engines will bring up dozens of companies that may be worth looking into. However, be wary of companies offering overnight or immediate results. These reports may be fraudulent or contain less information than you need.

Some Important Considerations

While employers are generally not allowed to refuse to hire people with criminal records, they are permitted to consider the relationship between the applicant's conviction record and the job being sought. For jobs with annual salaries of less than $75,000, consumer agencies are limited to providing information about a job applicant's arrests and conviction only during the last seven years.

If a credit report will be prepared, the applicant has the right to get a copy of that report. And if an applicant is not hired because of information found on a credit report, he or she must be given an opportunity to see the report. Because of frequent errors, the applicant may have a legitimate dispute about the data.

With today's ever-changing technology, Social Security theft is on the rise. During a Social Security check, an applicant's Social Security number is run through a government database to determine, for example, if the number is registered to that particular individual, if any other person has the same number, or if a name change has occurred.

From our experience, the data received on the report must be properly evaluated. Sometimes the report will indicate use of another Social Security number or another name associated with that number. In most cases this will probably be a family member who shared some kind of documentation such as a mortgage application or other credit application.

I-9 Form Requirements

Whenever an employer hires an individual (U.S. citizen or non-U.S. citizen) as an employee, the employer is required to complete an I-9 form. *If an employee does not have the proper documentation within three business days of his or her start date, the employer must terminate the employee.* If within this time the employee produces a receipt showing that he or she has applied for a work authorization or identification document, the employee must be given 90 days to produce the required documentation.

The employee must complete Section 1 at the time of hire (no later than the date the employee starts). It is the employer's responsibility to assure that the employee fills in the correct information and signs and dates the form. Failure to provide accurate information on the I-9 can make the employer liable.

The employee must present original documents (not photocopies) that establish identity and employment eligibility and may present the necessary documentation in one of two different ways:

1. Present one document from List A on the I-9 form, establishing both identity and employment eligibility; OR

2. Present one document from both List B (establishing identity) and List C (establishing employment eligibility) on the I-9 form.

The employer may not specify which documents an employee is required to present. Such a requirement can be considered "document abuse" and is an unlawful immigration-related employment practice. After reviewing the employee's documents, the employer must accept the documentation presented by the employee if the documents appear to be reasonably genuine. The completed I-9 forms are maintained in a separate management file and are not included in the employee file.

In some states and for government jobs, it may be a requirement to use the E-Verify website to determine the eligibility of the applicant to work in the United States. Check your state laws to determine if this step is required.

Other Final Steps

Once the selected applicant has accepted your offer, it is important to notify those you did not select. This notification should be timely and professional. You do this because it is common courtesy to do so. You also do it because it is good for your company image. The old adage about one person tells two and they each tell two and so on prevails even in this process. If you treat applicants badly, the word will get around and could damage future hiring efforts or even your customer relationships.

This notification, like all other notifications, should be in writing, letting them know they were not selected. The letters should not hurt them in any way and should leave their self-esteem intact. Thank them for their interest and the time they spent interviewing with your company. If they request specific details about why they were not selected, it is best to be noncommittal. Too many details can get you into trouble. It is best to state that *"All candidates were given full consideration, but one of the other candidates was more suited to our needs."* If you believe you may have future openings for which these applicants could qualify, let them know this, but don't create false hope.

Congratulations!

Well, you did it. You worked though all of the steps and you now have Grade AA talent on board.

We wish we could now tell you that all of the work is done, but it is just beginning. If you did not eliminate the rotten eggs before you started the process, Step 12 will help you complete that action and clear the way for your Grade AA talent. In the epilogue, we will give you insight into the processes for developing this top-performing candidate into a "golden egg" and making sure that he or she continues to be part of your workforce. Your competitive advantage depends on having a competent, stable, well-led workforce. The hiring process ensures that applicants are competent and the development process builds on that to create strong employees. Your efforts to retain that new employee focuses on creating the stability you need. The efforts you make as a manager and leader will bring it all together.

 On the accompanying CD-ROM you will find a Background Check Release Form and a Sample Letter of Non-Selection Following an Interview.

STEP 12
ELIMINATE THE
ROTTEN EGGS

STEP 12: ELIMINATE
THE ROTTEN EGGS

We set out to write *No More Rotten Eggs: A Dozen Steps to Grade AA Talent Management* to help owners and managers implement a disciplined process for finding the top performers that they need to be successful. The need for this process can come about in three different ways:

1. The best situation for any business is that they are growing and they need to add staff to deal with the added work requirements that come with growth.

2. Oftentimes, hiring is initiated because a valuable member of the team has left. They may have decided it is time to retire or they may need to deal with serious illness or take care of other family members that need assistance. Sometimes they leave to pursue a different career or job opportunity.

3. But frequently the reason that hiring was initiated is that there is someone on your current staff who really needs to be replaced. These are the rotten eggs who will hold you back because they don't fit or they don't care.

When you follow our process you will get people who do fit and they will care. But their ability to perform and demonstrate their capacity for greatness can be hampered by the presence of the rotten eggs we vowed not to hire anymore.

We have been making presentations on our hiring process to business owners and hiring managers for over 15 years. At the onset of the training session, we usually ask three questions to set the stage and to help us understand the status and goals of the attendees:

- First, how many of you in attendance are looking to add new staff in the next few months?

- Second, how many of you need to replace people who are leaving on their own accord?

- Third, how many of you currently have people on staff that you know you should replace right now?

Usually the first and second questions get a reasonably representative response; but the third question almost always gets a majority yes vote along with a few embarrassed smiles. The first 11 steps of this book dealt with helping owners and managers add new staff and ensure that each new hire possessed the skills, aptitudes, intelligence and personality to occupy those critical seats on the bus. We hope that you are going through the hiring process because of reason number one—you are growing and you need additional help. However, if you are hiring for reason number two—a need to replace someone leaving on their own accord, it is an opportunity to look for similar characteristics. If this is a top performer that you are replacing, then you will most likely want to clone this person. If you did not have any assessments done previously on the person who is leaving, we recommend that you do so before they leave so you can establish a benchmark for the personality, aptitude and emotional intelligence as well as the required skill sets. When you conduct interviews for the replacement, you can use those results as a benchmark for evaluating the applicants. This also is beneficial to use them as minimum level benchmarks so that you can upgrade the performance in the position.

Now, for those of you who are hiring because of reason number three—you need to replace someone currently on your staff, we have included Step 12 as part of the process. One of the most difficult and stressful activities in a business is the need to terminate employees. But as Jim Collins talks about in his book, *Good to Great*, it is just as important to make sure that you get the wrong people off the bus as it is to get the right people in the right seats on the bus. If you have employees that are not contributing to the success you seek or are, even worse, standing in the way of your success, it is absolutely essential that you deal with them. Because firing is stressful and fraught with potential legal problems, it must be accomplished with the same attention to detail and discipline as hiring.

The steps of the hiring process are designed to be sequential in nature with the exception of Step 12. We had hoped that before undertaking the search for Grade AA talent, you had terminated all the rotten eggs in your business. However, we are realists. We know all too well that many needed terminations are often delayed on the basis, "We couldn't afford to let him go until we had a replacement."

Whether you terminate before or after you hire the new person, it is absolutely critical to your business success that you ultimately do the deed. And the sooner it is done, the better it will be for all. However, even though the need to take this action is understood, there is usually delay, hesitation or procrastination. Why? Because firing is one of the most difficult things to do, unless it is done in anger or the heat of the moment. This, by the way, is never the time to do it.

Many of us will do just about anything to avoid the inevitable. Below are a few of the real reasons we tend to put off the inevitable:

1. **Denial.** We just can't admit that it is really necessary. After all, it is not the skills that are deficient. "She really knows her job." But the problem is that she often has a terrible attitude and cannot get along with her teammates. "But it is not every day. Maybe she will get over it." Face up to it. She is destroying cooperation and productivity and everyone will breathe easier when she is moved out.

2. **Fear of the unknown.** We've all worried about what would happen after we fire an employee. Debra personally was worried one time whether the person she fired that afternoon was going to beat her up in the parking lot that evening. In this turbulent economy there is also the fear of losing customers or other employees that your rotten egg knew and associated with.

3. **Emotional involvement.** In many cases we are firing employees that have been with us for some time and, in the course of that time, we have built a relationship with them. Debra had such an experience when she owned her printing company. She often speaks of it in her sessions, "Once I had to let a 12-year employee go; this was very disheartening. She had been my typesetter for many years. But with the advent of desktop publishing and computer to plate technology, she could not make the switch. So I hired another person who understood this new technology. But, rather than letting the existing typesetter go, I promoted her to a manager position. That was one of my worst decisions ever. Soon after I promoted her I realized she was missing a critical set of skills for this position. She did not have what it takes to manage or to deal with people. I had customers upset and employees ready to leave if this new manager remained. The end result was that I had to let her go despite the intense emotional involvement."

4. **Fear of a negative reflection on you.** Sure, we're always worried about how we're going to look in the eyes of our peers, customers, vendors and employees. It's very difficult to tell people that you had to fire the hotshot outside sales person you just hired six months ago.

5. **Possibility of legal action.** This is a genuine risk. We live in a lawsuit happy environment where there are some people who are always ready to sue. If you have taken the appropriate steps prior to the firing, then you are as ready

as you will ever be. Just do the termination. To minimize this risk, there are two actions that you should have taken:

First, your employee handbook must clearly identify that you are an at-will employer (Montana is the only state that does not recognize the at-will provisions). That means that either party (employee or employer) can terminate the relationship at any time without stating any justification.

Second, if you have decided to terminate for cause, then you must have a fully documented personnel file that demonstrates clear execution of the disciplinary process in your employee handbook. The offenses and the progressive application of disciplinary steps leading to the termination were fully documented; all interactions with the employee were acknowledged by the employee. The acknowledgement is intended to show that he was counseled, not necessarily that he agreed. Please note that this documentation must have been created when the incidents occurred and not from memory once termination is planned.

6. **Hope the problem will go away.** Good luck on that thought! This problem rarely, if ever, goes away by itself. Why would it? These people have it made where they are. Think about it—they are usually the one running the show and they know it. Why would they leave?

By not facing the inevitable as soon as possible you are creating more problems for yourself and for your business. If you have an employee who is not working out, everyone suffers: management, employees, the business and even the person who should be fired. The people that need to be fired will only drag you down. They drag your personal productivity down and they will affect everything you do. They drag down the morale of the company. They drag down the productivity of the department and therefore the company. They may even cost you money in poor quality, poor service, lost customers, etc. You will also lose respect from your employees by not firing this person or by taking too long to take action. Usually everyone knows this person needs to go and it only makes you look bad by not doing the deed.

There are many reasons that you need to be proactive in dealing with a firing and you shouldn't take it personally. You need to remember that these people are responsible for their own actions; therefore, the problems are of their own making. You need to prepare yourself psychologically for a firing, but you must also prepare administratively to ensure compliance with all governmental regulations.

Firing cannot be a knee-jerk reaction. Do not act impulsively or in a fit of anger. You need to prepare. Remember that you need to have a plan for anything you do. And the need for preparation is never more critical than when dealing with firings.

Make sure you have all the facts. Remember that there are at least two sides to every story. Never take one employee's story at face value about another employee. Check them out and make sure you have facts to back up the statements.

In some cases, it's difficult to make the firing decision because we need further justification that what we see or are struggling with is truly the way it is. In these situations, it's often justifiable to bring in an outside consultant or third party to observe and provide an unbiased opinion for you to hear.

In our book *How to Develop Top Performers*, we described the Interaction Report and the Counseling Report as tools for developing employees. These are also the forms you should use to document problems and record the plans for correction. We also discussed the progressive disciplinary process from warning to termination. As part of the plan for firing an employee you need to have that history, the audit trail that shows: 1) the pattern of problems and infractions; 2) the steps you have taken to help the employee rectify the situation; and 3) the results of your efforts and of the employee's efforts that show the ultimate conclusion that the situation is not improving.

Reminder: Make sure that copies of all written documents, as well as records of verbal communications, are kept in the employee's file. Anything that pertains to the problems that the employee caused should also be kept in the employee file. Along with the Employee Interaction and Counseling Reports, the file might also contain such things as:

- Complaints by peers, customers or vendors (written and/or notes of verbal complaints).

- Supporting documentation such as timesheets, production logs, records of missed deadlines, etc.

Important warning: Do not try to create these documents after you have fired the employee. If you enter a courtroom or arbitration with documents created from memory, you will lose your credibility.

Gilmore F. Diekmann, partner at Bronson, Bronson and McKinnon, San Francisco, has identified eight factors on which jurors base their findings of liability and determine large awards. These include the following:

1. Promises of long-term employment.

2. Failure to investigate properly before reaching a termination decision.

3. Failure to document poor performance or misconduct.

4. Failure to provide clear job descriptions, to define an employee's responsibilities and duties and expected levels of performance.

5. Subjective instead of objective evaluation criteria.

6. Inconsistent treatment of employees.

7. Absence of clear policies and procedures for resolving grievance and employee complaints.

8. Having different people establishing different expectations of performance levels. Have one person ultimately determine the standards. Too many cooks spoil the broth.

An owner/manager has a responsibility to help correct an employee's performance, within reason, primarily by letting the employee know there is a performance problem and giving them the opportunity to remedy the situation. If there has been sufficient history of problems and of attempts to correct the problems without success, then termination is justified.

Termination Requires Planning

Firings are emotional events, and they should be treated with consideration and forethought. The consequences of mishandling a firing can be unfortunate at the least.

 Once termination is decided to be the appropriate course of action, the actual firing must be planned. At the end of this step and on the accompanying CD your will find some forms that will be useful in planning and conducting the termination. We recommend that you start by reviewing the Termination Planning Checklist. This will help you assure compliance with employment laws. Then you should review the Termination Checklist. This will help you with planning the actions needed to complete the termination.

Major concerns for you to consider are:

- Who will do the firing?
- Who else needs to be informed before the firing?
- Where will it be done?
- When will it be done?
- What needs to be said to the person being terminated?

When it comes to who should do the deed, this is not a task that should be passed around. The best person to conduct the firing should be the employee's immediate supervisor or the person who had the immediate responsibility for this employee. Depending on the circumstances, it is often useful to have a third party present. Another supervisor or member of the human resources department would be appropriate, but a co-worker should not be involved.

Next, you need to decide where you are going to conduct the firing. The most important thing is that you always conduct this session in private. If the employee has his or her own office, then it may be the best spot because the employee can recover his or her composure in familiar surroundings. If that is not feasible, then select a neutral site that is close to the employee's area.

There are different opinions on when to do the firing. Some feel it's best at the beginning of the week; others say the end of the week. Those who favor the beginning say that it then allows the employee to begin actions to find a new job immediately. Those who favor the end say that it gives the employee the weekend to recover and plan for the future.

Personally, we have found Thursday to be a good day to let someone go with sufficient time left in the day for the employee to clear out his or her personal belongings, but late enough so that most of the other employees are gone and some embarrassment can be avoided. By letting the individual go on Thursday, you then have Friday to tell the staff what has happened and handle and questions or reactions that come up. The staff then has the weekend to digest the changes and return to work on Monday to start a fresh new week. The bottom line, however, is when you select the day and time, remember that it should be what will be the best for the employee, not what is best for the manager doing the firing.

Determining what to say needs to be thought out and planned ahead of time. This is also the time when less said is actually better. We recommend that you come up with a couple of sentences and stick to them. Create a mantra, if you will, and do not get hooked into a lot of other conversation. If you do engage in lengthy discussion, it often turns into a debate that is not useful to either the manager or the employee. It can also result in the manager saying too much, which can compromise the legality of the termination. Keeping it as simple as, "It is not working out and we have decided to make a change. We are letting you go today." This is in keeping with the "at-will" provisions and is usually enough to get the deed done. Despite any employee objections stick to the mantra. As difficult and as cold as this may seem, it is by far the safest and less stressful in the end.

The Termination Meeting

If everything on the checklists is in order, you need to prepare yourself for the actual meeting, including deciding the words that you will use. In preparing for this session, think about the following guidelines:

- Be straightforward. Be very clear about the reasons for the termination and be very clear that it is a termination.

- Be supportive. Encourage the employee to think of this as an opportunity to find something better suited to their skills.

- Allow the employee to speak, but don't get drawn into an argument.

- Be clear about the next actions such as turning in company property, clearing the desk, etc.

- Describe termination benefits such as severance pay, COBRA insurance, and outplacement services that are available.

- After the meeting, record exactly what happened and put these notes in the employee file.

Deal with the Stress

Terminations are stressful for everybody. Clearly the most stressed individual will be the person who was terminated, but the supervisor having to deal with the termination and the other employees will all be affected. It is important to set the rest of the employees at ease once the terminations have been conducted. Be open and honest about the reasons and reassure them that the company is moving forward. Do not demean the employees that have been terminated. Treat those employees who are negatively impacted with dignity, respect and support. It is the right thing to do, and it is an effective way of showing those who survive what kind of company they are working for and helping them begin to maintain positive feelings.

Bottom Line: Firing Employees—It Is Never Easy, But Sometimes It Is Necessary

One of the most difficult, stressful or distasteful tasks you may ever have to do is to fire someone. Your approach to firing needs to meet two critical criteria:

- It protects the dignity and the rights of the employee being terminated.

- It protects your company from retaliatory action by a disgruntled former employee.

Fire an employee the right way, and the stress is temporary. Fire them the wrong way, and you could experience some serious long-term consequences.

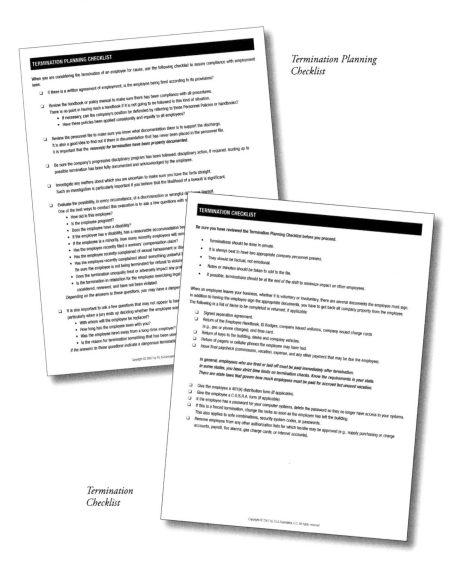

Termination Planning Checklist

Termination Checklist

No More Rotten Eggs • A Dozen Steps to Grade AA Talent Management

EPILOGUE
DEVELOP AND
RETAIN YOUR
GRADE AA TEAM

EPILOGUE: DEVELOP AND RETAIN YOUR GRADE AA TEAM

Our focus in *No More Rotten Eggs: A Dozen Steps to Grade AA Talent Management* was to create the infrastructure to take your company from good to great. You decided on the seats you needed on the bus and filled those seats with the people that were going to make a difference. You also took the actions to get the wrong people off the bus. But the total fulfillment of your vision depends on the actions that you take to integrate your new hires into the team in order to take full advantage of their talents.

There is an old saying that "The longest journey begins with a single step." This saying applies to many things we do—whether it is in our business life or our personal life. We especially believe it applies to the journey to make your newest hire an effective member of your organization. This journey begins the minute the new employee arrives for the first day of work and continues until the employee leaves your employment, ideally after a long and successful career. Every action that you as the owner or manager take must contribute to the growth of the employee. Every experience must provide lessons learned and help to avoid mistakes. Even the eventual mistake or error must be a basis for improvement and growth.

Although the process of developing top performers should be established and managed by the owner/manager, it is a team effort. It is not just a one-on-one activity. It involves everyone in the business in a cooperative effort that reinforces each employee's own plan for the future and ties it in effectively with the plans and goals of the company.

In our first efforts to define what it was we wanted to share with business owners, we developed a model of the process for success.

We intended it to apply to the process of running the business and delivering a product. Over time we found that it is useful in defining all levels and components of the business. When you think about it, basically everything starts with a plan and progresses through a logical sequence to success.

Thompson's Ten Principles for Success©

PEOPLE

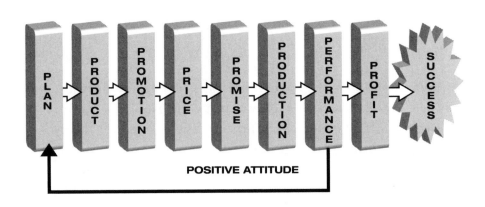

POSITIVE ATTITUDE

At first glance it may not appear to relate to developing employees, but take a moment and ponder what it says relative to developing a new hire into a successful top performer. It starts with the plan for the development that clearly outlines the steps and activities that will be followed. It has a product in mind, which is the top performer. There is promotion in the encouragement of high performance. It has a price both in the wage that the employee will earn and in the value he or she is expected to bring to the business. There are the mutual promises of owners, managers and employees that involve commitment. There is production, which in this case is the execution of the employee development plan. There is the performance evaluation of the employee and the processes employed in developing him or her into a top performer. Underlying it all are the people of the team and the attitudes they bring to the development process.

The development process is extensive, and we have created a second book, *How to Develop Top Performers*, that will address the actions needed to make this person a part of your team and to maximize his or her potential. It will provide the steps and the documentation that you need to make that happen. This book is designed to help you through the process. It becomes the plan that you will follow in the process of creating a top performer. Unlike the hiring process it is not sequential since all elements of the process must be employed concurrently. The key steps will outline the actions and processes that will be used. They will also demonstrate how they will contribute to the overall success of the employee.

If you are not sure why you should work so hard on the development process, just calculate what it cost you in time, energy and money to make the right hire. Then think of the benefits that this top performer will bring to your organization. Remember that top performing companies need top performing employees. The process begins with hiring the right person the first time; then taking the necessary steps to develop this person for success rather than failure; and finally, proactively strategizing to retain all your top performers.

The key elements of the development process are summarized below. They are fully described in *How to Develop Top Performers* along with all of the tools that you will need to complete the process.

Develop Your Top Performers—Ensure Their Success

Key 1: Orientation

Every journey has a beginning. The development of a top performer is no different. The startup is vital to creating the right atmosphere and establishing positive new relationships. The orientation must overcome the initial anxieties and ensure the employee feels welcome to his or her new team.

Key 2: The Employee Manual

The employee manual or handbook defines the company policies and practices. These help the employee understand his or her entitlements as well as the "rules of the game" and begin the process of team building and employee "ownership."

Key 3: Procedure Manuals

The employee manual provides the policies. The procedure manual provides the step-by-step actions to adhere to polices, to build the product and to satisfy both the internal and the external customers.

Key 4: Training

No matter how skilled the new hire is, there is always the need for training. This runs the gamut from the hard skills called for in the job description to the soft skills needed for successful team building for management and leadership.

Key 5: Performance Evaluations

Every process needs to have those events where we evaluate our progress and ensure our journey is progressing as it should. The performance appraisal is essential to checking status as well as providing career direction and improvement.

Key 6: Disciplinary Actions

Every journey has a few bumps. The disciplinary process—like the performance evaluation—helps to point out the areas needing improvement, and it defines the actions that need to be accomplished and the consequences of not achieving those expected levels of performance.

Master Key: It's Your Responsibility

When it comes to developing top performers, the owners and managers must recognize that "the buck stops here." They alone are responsible for the successful pursuit of the development process and the integration of all of their top performers into a cohesive team.

Retaining Your Grade AA Talent

Now that you've developed your recent hire into the top performer that you wanted, it is time to take the actions that are going to keep that person as part of your team. If the reason that you followed the hiring process was to replace someone valuable that left, then you know firsthand the importance of a proactive retention policy. Workforce stability is needed for future growth. And your customers evaluate it as a measure of your own capability.

There have been many books and articles on the subject of retention and what it takes to keep employees happy. One of the best resources is *The 100 Best Companies to Work for in America*, by Robert Levering and Milton Moskowitz. *Fortune* magazine has also reported the results of its surveys on the best companies to work for. The prevailing theme in all of these studies is associated with several key factors:

- Employee well-being is central to the company values
- The company provides a reasonable commitment to job security
- Facilities are clearly people-friendly
- The company is committed to helping employees achieve balance in their work and their personal lives
- Employee empowerment is a major driver in the company operations
- Open lines of communication are maintained
- The employees have a sense of ownership in the company

The challenge is clearly set for every business to be exciting, fun, and supportive of the employee's goals, ambitions and family. In *How to Retain Top Performers* we will help you rise up to these challenges and develop the strategies that will make retention of top performers easier to achieve. In developing these strategies, we used as a major reference *Keeping Good People*, by Roger E. Herman. His book is subtitled *Strategies for Solving the #1 Problem Facing Business Today*.

It is important you realize that finding, developing and retaining Grade AA talent is your most critical activity. In 2009, while we saw tremendous increases in the unemployment rate, most companies that tried to upgrade their staff found that hiring still continued to be difficult. The applicants did not possess the critical skills and intelligence needed to cope with dramatically increasing technology. In addition, in the years leading up to 2020, we will see the impact of retiring Baby Boomers and the smaller following generations, so it will be essential to focus on retention of your top performers and execution of disciplined and aggressive hiring processes. This will lead to the success of your business.

Our consulting takes us into many different companies. It is immediately evident which companies have understood and implemented the strategies for retention. In these cases, employee morale is high and the quality of the product is good. Also, the owners/managers clearly understand their personal capabilities and have taken their optimal role in the company. The combination of these factors is producing growth while maintaining harmony in the workplace and, most importantly, resulting in a stable competent workforce. The result is a competitive advantage for the company and a multiplier in productivity and quality.

The prevailing theme in *How to Retain Top Performers* is communication in all directions. It is paramount that we understand how to communicate and that we apply the principles of listening and encouraging feedback. We must also develop the tools and mediums to keep everyone informed within our particular organization. Information is the vital lifeblood of the company, and it keeps everyone on track. For owners and managers it is the clearest manifestation of their leadership.

General Colin Powell stated it this way:

"The day soldiers stop bringing you their problems is the day you have stopped leading them. They have either lost confidence that you can help them or concluded that you do not care. Either case is a failure of leadership."

General Powell goes on to explain: *"If this were a litmus test, the majority of CEOs would fail. One, they build so many barriers to upward communication that the very idea of someone lower in the hierarchy looking up to the leader is ludicrous. Two, the corporate culture they foster often defines asking for help as weakness or failure, so people cover up their gaps, and the organization suffers accordingly. Real leaders make themselves accessible and available. They show concern for the efforts and challenges faced by underlings—even as they demand high standards. Accordingly they are more likely to create an environment where problem analysis replaces blame."*

That is what it's all about. To continue being successful in your business you must create an environment that promotes the retention of your top performers.

The key elements of the retention process are summarized below. They are fully developed in *How to Retain Top Performers* along with all of the tools that you will need to complete the process.

Retain Your Top Performers—Ensure Your Success

Key 1: Become an Employer of Choice.

There is reason to worry about retention of top performers. Companies try to understand the underlying reasons why employees leave and what it will take to retain the staff they have worked hard to hire and develop. The process to become an employer of choice needs to be understood and used in order to survive today.

Key 2: Communication.

How do you deal with issues if you don't know how to talk about them? It is important that you understand the barriers to effective communication and employ the tools that are needed to make every communication effective.

Key 3: Empowerment.

Employees want the authority that is commensurate with their responsibilities. If they are going to be effective members of the company, they want to know how the company works and how they can independently contribute to its success. Empowerment makes the business function smoothly and with purpose.

Key 4: Motivate/Energize.

You live in a high-tempo world, and you need to instill in your employees the desire and the energy to deal with their duties and responsibilities. While most people have their own motivators, you may need to make those coincide with the goals of the company.

Key 5: Strategies for Retention.

Employee retention does not just happen. It must be strategized and plans must be developed. In today's environment, we must consider all the facets of the business life and address those in our employee retention plan.

Master Key: Successful Team Building Begins with You!

Retention of top performers begins at the top. It is the actions of the owner/manager and the environment they create that will determine success.

BIBLIOGRAPHY

Bliss, Wendy. *Legal, Effective References: How to Give and Get Them.* Alexandria, VA: Society for Human Resource Management, 2001.

Buckingham, Marcus, and Clifton, Donald. *Now, Discover Your Strengths.* New York: The Free Press, 2001.

Buckingham, Marcus, and Coffman, Curt. *First Break All the Rules: What the World's Greatest Managers Do Differently.* New York: Simon & Schuster, 1999.

Collins, James C. *Good to Great: Why Some Companies Make the Leap . . . and Others Don't.* New York: HarperCollins, 2001.

Dinterman, Walter A. *Zero Defect Hiring: A Quick Guide to the Most Important Decisions Managers Have to Make.* San Francisco, CA: Pfeiffer, 2003.

Fein, Richard. *101 Hiring Mistakes Employers Make . . . and How to Avoid Them.* Manassas Park, VA: Impact Publications, 2000.

Freiberg, Kevin, and Freiberg, Jackie. *Nuts! Southwest Airlines' Crazy Recipe for Business and Personal Success.* Austin, TX: Bard Press, 1996.

George, William. *Authentic Leadership: Rediscovering the Secrets to Creating Lasting Value.* San Francisco, CA: Jossey-Bass, 2003.

Goleman, Daniel, and Cherniss, Cary. *The Emotionally Intelligent Workplace: How to Select for, Measure, and Improve Emotional Intelligence in Individuals, Groups, and Organizations.* San Francisco, CA: Jossey-Bass, 2001.

Goleman, Daniel. *Working with Emotional Intelligence.* New York: Bantam Books, 1998.

Greenberg, Herb; Weinstein, Harold; and Sweeney, Patrick. *How to Hire and Develop Your Next Top Performer: The Five Qualities That Make Salespeople Great.* New York: McGraw-Hill, 2001.

Hacker, Carol A. *The Costs of Bad Hiring Decisions & How to Avoid Them.* Boca Raton, FL: St. Lucie Press, 1996.

Harris, Jim, and Brannick, Joan. *Finding & Keeping Great Employees.* New York: AMA Publications, 1999.

Harvard Business Review on Finding and Keeping the Best People. Boston, MA: Harvard Business School, 1994, 2000, 2001.

Hendrickson, Thomas M. *Personal Profile Analysis: A Technical Manual.* Marlow, England: Thomas International Limited, 1983.

Herman, Roger, and Gioia, Joyce. *Lean & Meaningful: A New Culture for Corporate America.* Winchester, VA: Oakhill Press, 1998.

Herman, Roger, and Gioia, Joyce. *Workforce Stability: Your Competitive Edge: How to Attract, Optimize, and Hold Your Best Employees.* Winchester, VA: Oakhill Press, 2000.

Herman, Roger; Olivo, Tom; and Gioia, Joyce. *Impending Crisis: Too Many Jobs, Too Few People.* Winchester, VA: Oakhill Press, 2003.

Horowitz, Alan. *The Unofficial Guide to Hiring and Firing People.* New York: Macmillan, 1999.

Irvine, Sidney. *Personal Profile Analysis: The Technical Resource Book.* Marlow, England: Thomas International Limited, 2003.

Kleiman, Mel, and Kleiman, Brent. *Recruit Smarter, Not Harder: A Simple Story That Reveals the Powerful Truths About Recruiting the Best Hourly Employees.* Houston, TX: HTG Press, 2002.

Kleiman, Mel. *Hire Tough, Manage Easy: How to Find and Hire the Best Hourly Employees.* Houston, TX: Humetrics Press, 1999.

Klinvex, Kevin; O'Connell, Matthew; and Klinvex, Christopher. *Hiring Great People.* New York: McGraw-Hill, 1999.

Leuner, P. "Emotional Intelligence and Emancipation." *Praxis der Kinderpsychologie und Kinderpsychiatrie* 15 (1966): 196–203.

Messmer, Max. *Human Resources Kit for Dummies.* Foster City, CA: IDG Books Worldwide, 1999.

Mornell, Pierre. *45 Effective Ways for Hiring Smart! How to Predict Winners and Losers in the Incredibly Expensive People-Reading Game.* Berkeley, CA: Ten Speed Press, 1998.

Outlaw, Wayne. *Smart Staffing: How to Hire, Reward, and Keep Top Employees for Your Growing Company.* Chicago, IL: Upstart Publishing, 1998.

Peters, Tom, and Austin, Nancy. *A Passion for Excellence: The Leadership Difference.* New York: Warner Books, 1985.

Rueff, Rusty, and Stringer, Hank. *Talent Force: A New Manifesto for the Human Side of Business.* Upper Saddle River, NJ: Prentice Hall, 2006.

Smart, Bradford D. *Top Grading: How Leading Companies Win by Hiring, Coaching, and Keeping the Best People.* New York: Penguin Group, 1999, 2005.

Stein, Steven, and Book, Howard. *The EQ Edge: Emotional Intelligence and Your Success.* Mississauga, ON, Canada: Jossey-Bass, 2000, 2006.

User's Manual for the WPT and SLE. Libertyville, IL: Wonderlic, Inc., 2002.

Wetherbe, James C. *The World on Time: The 11 Management Principles That Made FedEx an Overnight Sensation.* Santa Monica, CA: Knowledge Exchange, 1996.

Winninger, Thomas. *Hiring Smart: How to Hire a Team That Wants to Work.* Rocklin, CA: Prima Publishing, 1997.

END-USER LICENSE AGREEMENT

Please carefully read this End-User License Agreement ("Agreement") before installing or using the No More Rotten Eggs CD-ROM on your PC. The right to use the CD-ROM is granted by TG & Associates, LLC to you only on the condition that you agree to its terms. Please note that installing or using the CD-ROM indicates your acceptance of these terms and conditions.

1. Copyright Ownership

You acknowledge that all copyrights and other intellectual property rights in the CD-ROM are owned by TG & Associates, LLC. The contents of the CD-ROM are protected under the copyright law of the USA.

2. Grant of License

(1) Subject to the conditions of the Agreement, TG & Associates, LLC grants to you a non-exclusive right to use the CD-ROM. You may install and use the information on the CD-ROM.

(2) You may make a copy of the contents of the CD-ROM for backup and storage purpose.

(3) You may make copies of the contents of the CD-ROM for personal and individual use, without limitation of volume, and utilize such copies, provided that each such copy contains copyright and/or other proprietary rights notice in the same manner as appeared on the CD-ROM.

3. Restriction

(1) You may not copy or use the contents of the CD-ROM, in whole or in part, other than as expressly specified in this Agreement.

(2) You have no right to grant a license to any other company to use the contents of the CD-ROM, and may not sell, lease or rent the CD-ROM to any other person for any purpose.

4. Limited Warranty

The CD-ROM and its contents are provided "as is" without warranty of any kind. Should there be any problem arising from or caused by the CD-ROM and its contents, you should settle all such problems at your own costs and responsibilities. If there is a readability issue with the CD-ROM, TG & Associates will replace the defective CD-ROM.

5. Term

This Agreement will become effective on the date when you open the package and install the CD-ROM onto your machine, and continue to be in effect until terminated. You may terminate the agreement by returning the CD-ROM. TG & Associates will terminate the agreement if you fail to comply with any provision of the agreement.

6. U.S. Government User

If you are an agency of the United States of America (the "Government"), you acknowledge TG & Associates' representation that the CD-ROM is a "Commercial Item" as defined in Federal Acquisition Regulation (FAR) part 2.101 (g) and is only licensed to you with the same use rights TG & Associates grants all commercial end users pursuant to the terms of this Agreement.

7. General

(1) No modification, change, addition, deletion or other alteration of or to the Agreement will be valid unless reduced to writing and signed by an authorized representative of TG & Associates, LLC.

(2) Even if any part of the Agreement is held invalid by or in conflict with any law having jurisdiction over this Agreement, the remaining provisions will remain in full force and effect.

(3) The Agreement shall be governed by and interpreted under the laws of the USA.

INDEX

Absenteeism, 117
Acceptance
  deadlines for, 135
  of offer letters, 136
Accidents on the job, 142
Active job seekers, 45
ADA (Americans with Disabilities
  Act), 63
Adaptability, 111–12
Advertising
  with blind ads, 55
  newspaper, 46–47, 54
  television, 54
Age, 89
Allport, Gordon, 31
Americans with Disabilities Act
  (ADA), 63
Annual Applicant Statistics, 143
Anti-Discrimination Guidelines, 66,
  75, 84–85, 87, 89–93, 96
Applicant Tracking System (ATS)
  prescreening with, 63
  for recruitment, 57
Application forms, 13–14, 73–79, 85
  for drivers, 78
  EEOC-compliant, 75–76
  as legal documents, 73–75, 77
  prescreening, 76–77
  retention requirements for, 79
Arrest records, 89
Arrest warrants, 145
Assertiveness, 111
ATS. See Applicant Tracking System
Attendance, 92
At-will employment, 76, 135, 155
At-will provisions, 160
Audit reports, 106–8

Background Check Release Form,
  148
Background checks, 135, 143–45
Bar-On, Reuven, 109, 110
Bar-On EQ-i®, 112–13

Behavioral characteristics overview
  chart, 36
Behavioral competencies, 24
Behavioral expectations, 29–41
  DISC system for, 30–33
  Human Job Analysis for, 37–41
  and Marston's model of behavior
    chart, 33
  psychology of profiling for, 30–32
  Thomas System profiling for,
    34–36
Behavioral-based interview questions,
  105–6
Behaviors, 1
Benefits packages, 135
Big Five (Five Factor Model), 31
Birth dates, 89
Birthplace, 89
Blind ads, 55
Body language, 94
Bonuses, 135

Call center audit report, 106
Canadian Human Rights Act, 30,
  104
Candidate Evaluation Form, 95, 96
Candidate feedback report, 106
Candidate pool
  and labor crisis, 10
  and recruitment, 45
Career counseling centers, 51
Career guide report, 106
Career web page, 52–53
CareerBuilder.com, 47, 54, 63, 65
Career-day functions, 51
Chronic absenteeism, 117
Citizenship, 90
Classified Ad Placement Log, 57
Classified Ad Placement Request
  Form, 57
Classified advertisements, 56–57
Cognitive testing, 101–2
Cohesive company culture, 88

College newspapers, 47
Collins, Jim, 3, 20, 152
Common sense, 110
Communication, 172
  by email, 61, 63–64, 68–69
  and employee retention, 170–71
  by telephone, 119, 120
  during termination meetings, 160
  verbal, 137, 157
  written, 68–69, 119, 134, 148,
    157
Company culture, 88
Company growth, 99–100, 151
Company website, 50, 52–53
Comparison report, 106, 108
Compatibility report, 106
Compensation information
  in job advertisements, 57
  in offer letters, 133–35
Compliance
  on application forms, 75–76
  in DISC system, 33
  with terminations, 156
Comprehension testing, 101–2
Confidentiality, 135
Contract for employment, 135
Conviction records, 89, 145–46
Cooperative testing, 104–13
Coordination, 101
Corporate Leadership Council, 2
Counseling Report, 156–57
Craigslist, 56
Credit history, 90, 145
Credit reports, 146
Criminal history, 145
Culture, company, 88
Customer referrals, 49–50
Customer service audit reports, 107

Deadlines, acceptance, 135
Decision matrix, for evaluation of
    candidates, 127–29
Decision Matrix Form, 129
Denial, 153
Department of Commerce, 1
Department of Labor, 1
Diekmann, Gilmore F., 157

Disability, 90, 102
DISC system
  for cooperative testing, 104
  and Human Job Analysis, 37–41
  and Personal Profile Analysis, 34,
    35
  profiling based on, 30–33
Disciplinary actions, 156–57, 168
Discipline problems, 117
Discrimination, 77
Disqualifiers, in reference checks, 121
Diversity, team, 99–100
Documentation, for terminations,
    155–57
Dominance (DISC system), 33
"Dozen Steps to Grade AA Talent
    Management," 12–15
Driver application forms, 78
Driving records, 145
Drucker, Peter, 1
Drug testing, 135, 141–43
Drug-Free Workplace Advisor
    Program Builder, 142

Education, 90, 145
EEOC. See Equal Employment
    Opportunity Commission
Effective management report, 107
Email, 61, 63–64, 68–69
Emergency notifications, 91
Emotional intelligence, 108–13
Emotional involvement, 154
Emotional Quotient (EQ), 110–12
Emotions of Normal People, The
    (William Moulton Marston), 31
Empathy, 111
Employee development,
    165–69
Employee manuals, 168
Employee morale, 170
Employee orientation, 167
Employee Referral Form, 49–50
Employee referral programs, 49
Employee retention, 169–73
  communication for, 170–71
  factors in, 169–70
  steps for, 171–73

Employees, 49
  replacement of, 152
  and terminations, 161
"Employer of choice," 171–72
Employment, at-will, 76, 135, 155, 160
Employment agencies, 48
Employment applications. *See* Application forms
Employment contract, 135
Employment discrimination, 77
Employment opportunities web page, 52–53
Empowerment, 169, 172
Ending interviews, 94–95
EQ (Emotional Quotient), 110–12
Equal Employment Opportunity Commission (EEOC)
  compliant application forms, 75–76
  and prescreening questions, 63, 89
  and testing candidates, 113
  and Thomas Personality Profiling System, 30, 104
Equipment testing, 102–3
Etiquette, 65
Evaluation of candidates, 14, 125–29
  decision matrix for, 127–28
  and halo effect, 127–28
  steps in, 125–26
  timeliness in, 129
E-verify, 147
Executive summary report, 107
Expectations. *See* Behavioral expectations

Facebook, 86
Failed hires, 4, 128
Fair Credit Reporting Compliance, 144
Fair Labor Standards Act (FLSA), 26, 79
Falsification of information
  on application forms, 73
  and background checks, 143
  on I-9 forms, 147

Federal restrictions, on interview questions, 88
Felony convictions, 145
Final checks, 14–15, 141–48
  background checks, 143–45
  conviction records, 145–46
  drug testing, 141–43
  I-9 Forms, 146–47
  non-selected candidates, 147–48
Financial status, 90
Firing employees. *See* Terminations
First impressions, 86–87, 95
Five Factor Model (Big Five), 31
Flexibility, 112
FLSA (Fair Labor Standards Act), 26, 79
Following up (to offer letters), 136
Four Quadrant Behavior (4QB), 30

Gender, 93
General interview questionnaire report, 107
General mood, 112
Go Jobing Magazine, 3, 9–10
Good to Great (Jim Collins), 3, 20, 152
Google, 86
Growth of company, 99–100, 151

"Halo effect," 127–28
Happiness, 112
Hendrickson, Thomas, 31, 108
Herman, Roger E., 170
Hippocrates, 30
Hiring. *See also* Evaluation of candidates
  goals and objectives in, 100, 151–52
  hesitation in, 129
  non-discriminatory, 75–76
  process of, 10–11
HJA. *See* Human Job Analysis
How to Develop Top Performers (Debra Thompson and Bill Greif), 156–57, 167
How to Retain Top Performers (Debra Thompson and Bill Greif), 169

Human Equation, The (Jeffrey Pfeffer), 2
Human Job Analysis (HJA), 13, 37–41
Human side of business, 4

I-9 Form
    falsifying information on, 147
    incomplete, 146
Icebreaker questions, 93
Impulse control, 112
Independence, 111
Influence (DISC system), 33
InfoLink Screening Services, 143
Informed hiring decisions, 113, 128
Infrastructure review, 20–21
Instruments for testing, 114
Intelligence Quotient (IQ), 109
Interaction Report, 156–57
Internal customer concept, 19
Internet job boards, 52–56
Internet newspaper ads, 46–47
Internship programs, 51
Interpersonal capacity, 111
Interpersonal relationship, 111
Interview Response Form, 94, 96
Interviews, 14, 83–96
    anti-discrimination guidelines for, 89–93
    behavioral-based questions for, 105–6
    effective, 93–95
    first impressions in, 86–87
    panel, 88
    with peers, 87–88
    preparation for, 84–86
    prescreening for, 67
    restrictions on questions in, 88–93
    and social media sites, 86
    structured, 83–84
IQ (Intelligence Quotient), 109

Jackson, Douglas Northrop, 31
Job Assessment Worksheet, 20, 23–24
Job boards, 52–56

Job descriptions, 13, 19–26
    creation of, 22–23
    format of, 24–25
    infrastructure review for, 20–21
    for interviews, 85, 93–94
    in offer letter, 134
    prescreening with, 61
    reassessment of existing, 23–24
Job functions, 20
Job offers, 14, 133–37
    acceptance of, 136
    letters for, 133–36
    making changes to, 137
    rejection of, 136–37
    verbal, 133
Job requirements, 19–21
Job responsibilities, 57
Job titles, 134
Jung, Carl Gustav, 30
Junior Achievement programs, 51
Justification, of termination, 156–57

Keeping Good People (Roger E. Herman), 170

Labor crisis, 3, 170
Lawsuits, 118, 154–55
Legal documentation, 73–75, 77
Legal problems
    with poor hiring decisions, 118
    with terminations, 153, 157–58
Length of employment, 135
Letter of Non-Selection Following an Interview, 148
Levering, Robert, 169
Liability, in terminations, 157–58
Licenses, professional, 145
Losses due to theft, 117
Lowering the bar, 70, 76

Management reports, 107
Manager responsibility, 168–69, 172
Managerial positions, 108–9
Manuals, 168
Marital status, 91
Marshall, Ian, 3

Marston, William Moulton, 31, 34
Mathematics testing, 101–2
Mayer, Jack, 110
McKinsey & Company, 2
Meetings, termination, 160–61
Mentor programs, 51
Military records, 91
Military service verification, 145
Millionaire Mind, The (Thomas
    Stanley), 109
Model of Behavior Chart, 33
Monster.com, 47, 53–54, 63, 65
Morale, employee, 170
Moskowitz, Milton, 169
Motivation, 172
Motor vehicle driving records, 145
Murray, Henry, 31
MySpace, 86

Names, questions about, 91
National Institute of Occupational
    Safety and Health, 1
National origin, 90
Need Theory, Murray's, 31
Negotiation, of job offers, 137
Networking, 50–51
Newsletters, 47
Newspaper advertising
  in college papers, 48
  on Internet, 46–47
  print vs. online, 54
"No-hire" application forms, 79
Non-discriminatory hiring, 75–76
Non-selected candidates, 68–69,
    147–48
Note taking, 94

Occupational Safety and Health
    Administration (OSHA),
    141–42
Offer letters, 133–36
  acceptance of, 136
  compensation defined in, 133–35
  rejection of, 136–37
  sending, 136
  terms and conditions in, 134–35

Offers. *See* Job offers
*100 Best Companies to Work for in
    America, The* (Robert Levering
    and Milton Moskowitz), 169
Online prescreening, 63–64
Online recruitment, 51–56
  CareerBuilder, 54
  company websites, 52–53
  Craigslist, 56
  Monster.com, 53–54
  RegionalHelpWanted.com, 53
  TG & Associates' Job Board, 55
Optimism, 112
Organization charts, 20
Organizational affiliations, 92
Orientation, employee, 167
OSHA (Occupational Safety and
    Health Administration),
    141–42

Panel interviews, 88
Passive job seekers, 45
"Pay and pray" method, 46
Payscale.com, 134
Peer interviews, 87–88
Performance evaluations, 168
Perks, 135
Personal Profile Analysis (PPA),
    31–32, 34, 105
Personal references, 119
Personality Domains, Jackson's, 31
Personality profiling, 30–36
  and candidate testing, 104–8
  and company growth, 99–100
  and Marston's model of behavior
    chart, 33
  psychology of, 30–32
  and reference checks, 120
  Thomas System, 34–36
Pfeffer, Jeffrey, 2
Phone etiquette, 65
Physical examinations, 135
Powell, Colin, 171
PPA (Personal Profile Analysis),
    31–32, 34, 105
Prejudices, setting aside, 87

Preparation
    for interviews, 84–86
    for reference checks, 120
    for terminations, 158–60
Prescreening, 13, 61–70
    of non-selected candidates, 68–69
    online, 54, 63–64
    over the phone, 64–66, 85
    questionnaires for, 63–64, 85
    of resumes, 61–62
    of selected candidates, 68
    steps in, 67
Previous employers, 145
Print media, 46–48
Privacy
    for interviews, 93
    in prescreening, 64
    for terminations, 159
Private investigators, 145
Problem-solving, 112
Procedure manuals, 168
Procrastination, of terminations,
    153–56
Professional licenses, 145
Promises, 135
Psychology, 30–32
Public appearances, 50–51
Public records, 145
Punctuality, 92

Questionnaires
    for interviews, 85
    for prescreening, 63–64, 85
    Thomas Personality Profiling
        System, 105
Questions
    about names, 91
    behavioral-based, 105–6
    icebreaker, 93
    legal restrictions on, in interviews,
        88–93
    prescreening, 54, 65–66
    tailored, 85

Race, 92
Raises, 135

Rating system, 126
Reality testing, 112
Recruiting agencies, 48
Recruitment, 13, 45–57
    from within, 48–49
    agencies for, 48
    applicant tracking systems for, 57
    and candidate pool, 45
    classified ads for, 56–57
    and networking, 50–51
    online, 51–56
    in print media, 46–48
    and referrals, 49–50
    from schools and universities, 51
    with Welcome Wagon services, 51
Red flags
    on application forms, 75, 76–77
    on reference checks, 119–20
    on resumes, 62
Reference Checking Form, 122
Reference checks, 14, 117–22
    for currently employed candidates,
        119
    importance of, 117, 119–20
    objectives for, 117–18
    possible disqualifiers in, 121
    preparation for, 120
    steps in, 119–21
References
    personal, 119
    unwilling, 121
Referrals, 49–50
RegionalHelpWanted.com, 53
Rejections, of job offers, 136–37
Release forms, 75, 118, 135, 144
Reliability, 92
Religion, 92
Relocation arrangements, 56, 135
Replacement, of current employees,
    152
Reports
    background check, 144–45
    counseling, 156–57
    credit, 146
    interaction, 156–57
    management, 107

Personal Profile Analysis, 105
Thomas Personality Profiling
    System, 106–8, 114
Request for Verification of
    Employment, 119, 122
Residence, 93
Resumes, 61–62
Retention, of application forms, 79
Return on investment (ROI), 3
Rueff, Rusty, 16

SAID (Substance Abuse Information
    Database), 142
Salary statistics, 134
Salary.com, 134
Sales audit report, 107
Sales interview questionnaire report,
    107
Salovey, Peter, 110
Schools, 51
Scouting programs, 51
Screening application forms, 76–77
Security clearance, 135
Security companies, 145
Selected candidates, 68
Self-actualization, 111
Self-awareness, 111
Self-regard, 111
Sex (gender), 93
Skills, 1, 29
Social media sites, 86
Social responsibility, 111
Social Security numbers, 145, 146
Soft skills, 29
Staffing agencies, 48
Standardization, of application
    forms, 74–75
Stanley, Thomas, 109
Start date, 134, 136
State restrictions, on interview
    questions, 88
Static traits, 110
Steadiness (DISC system), 33
Stereotypes, 87
Strategic traits, 110
Street smarts, 110
Strengths and limitations summary
    report, 108

Stress
    as emotional intelligence, 112
    and office behavior, 105
    and terminations, 161–62
Stress management, 112
Stress tolerance, 112
Stringer, Hank, 16
Structured Interview Checklist, 86,
    96
Structured Interview Questions,
    96
Structured interviews, 83–84
Substance abuse, 141–43
Substance Abuse Information
    Database (SAID), 142
Success criteria, 38

Tailored questions, 85
Talent Force (Rusty Rueff and Hank
    Stringer), 16
Team diversity, 99–100
Technical and administrative audit
    report, 108
Telephone
    communication by, 119, 120
    etiquette, 65
    prescreening by, 64–66, 69
Telephone Prescreening Form, 66
Telephone Reference Checking form,
    120
Television advertising, 54
"Temp-to-perm" agreement, 48
Termination benefits, 161
Termination Checklist, 158
Termination meetings, 160–61
Termination Planning Checklist,
    158
Terminations, 151–62
    and hiring goals, 151–52
    for I-9 non-completion, 146
    justification of, 156–57
    and legal liability, 157–58
    planning for, 158–60
    proactive, 156
    procrastination of, 153–56
    stresses of, 161–62
Terms and conditions (of job offers),
    133–35

Testing, 14, 99–114
  cognitive, 101–2
  drug, 135, 141–43
  for emotional intelligence, 108–13
  for equipment operation, 102–3
  and hiring objectives, 100
  instruments for, 114
  and objectivity, 113
  personality profiling, 104–8
  and team diversity, 99–100
TG & Associates' Job Board, 55
Theft
  Social Security, 146
  workplace, 117, 118
Thomas Personality Profiling System,
  30, 34–36, 104–8, 114
Thompson's Ten Principles for
  Success, 9
Timeliness
  in evaluation of candidates, 129
  in hiring process, 10
  with non-selected candidates,
    68–69, 147
Top performers, 3–4, 166–67
Top 20 Interview Questions, 85, 96
Tours, company, 51
Trade secrets agreements, 135
Training, 76, 168
Training needs analysis report, 108
Trait Measurement, Allport's, 31

Unemployables, 45
University career counseling centers,
  51
Unwilling references, 121
U.S. Bureau of Labor Statistics, 134
U.S. Department of Labor, 142

Vacations, 135
Vendor referrals, 50
Verbal communication, 137, 157
Verbal job offers, 133
Verification of information, 117–18
Violence, workplace, 117, 118

Wagner, Richard, 109
"War for Talent," 2
Warning signs. See Red flags
Website, company, 50, 52–53
Weighting, candidate, 125–26
Welcome Wagon services, 51
Wonderlic Personnel Test-Revised
  (WPT-R), 101–3, 108–9
Workforce stability, 3
Working conditions, 57
Working Partners for an Alcohol-
  and Drug-Free Workplace, 142
Workplace theft, 117, 118
Workplace violence, 117, 118
Written communication, 68–69, 119,
  134, 148, 157

CONGRATULATIONS!

You have finished the book. Now you are ready to implement the dozen steps to get rid of your rotten eggs and recruit Grade AA talent!

Contact Debra and Bill at TG & Associates (877.842.7762) for the tools and products described in *No More Rotten Eggs* and for other services to help you with A Dozen Steps to Grade AA Talent Management.

Use this Hiring Checklist to select what you need:

❑ **Step 1: Define the Job—Job Description**—Having trouble creating a Job Description? Call TG & Associates to create one. Visit their website, www.tgassociates.com, to see if one has already been created!

❑ **Step 3: Recruit—Internet Ads**—TG & Associates offers assistance in placing ads on national job boards such as Monster and CareerBuilder. They can also create a tailored internet ad to attract Grade AA talent.

❑ **Step 7: Test—Testing and Assessments**—TG & Associates offers all the assessments mentioned in the book (Personality Profile Reports, Behavioral Based Interview Questions, Wonderlic Testing and Emotional Intelligence Testing. Just call to order! Mention you got referred from the book to get $10 off a profile.

❑ **Step 8: Reference Check**—Not getting the information you want to know about your candidate's prior jobs? Ask TG & Associates to get it for you!

❑ **Step 11: Final Checks—Background Checks**—DO NOT perform background checking yourself. Use a professional firm, or it can cost you! The CD-ROM includes a background release form for you to fax back to TG & Associates at 520.751.7515. It's that simple! Mention the book to get $15 off the background check.

If you think that hiring is too much work and you don't have the time to devote to recruit Grade AA talent yourself, don't shortcut the process. Let TG & Associates do it for you! Call TG & Associates for more information (877.842.7762).

ABOUT THE AUTHORS

Debra Thompson, President of TG & Associates, LLC, is an international speaker, consultant, coach and author. TG & Associates specializes in *the human side of business* by providing human resource services and customized recruiting services for small businesses throughout the U.S. and Canada.

Debra started in the graphics industry in 1977 as a typesetter. She became a franchisee of American Speedy Printing with a company located in Orchard Lake, Michigan. She owned and operated that franchise until 1994. In addition she served as a new owner trainer for American Speedy, whose headquarters was close to her store. Over time American Speedy morphed into Allegra Network, which remains one of her major clients

In 1995 Debra and Bill founded TG & Associates with a principal focus in the graphics industry. Debra initially focused on customer service training, but it became quickly apparent that the real need was people management skills. She devoted her energies to understanding what it takes to hire, develop and retain top performers and in turn to train business owners and managers to be successful people-managers. To that end she was able to have specialized one-on-one training with Dr. Tom Hendrickson who created the Thomas Personality Profile Analysis. Debra was certified to read and interpret the Thomas DISC profile, which became the key instrument in her coaching and teambuilding work.

Debra with Bill's help created *Thompson's Ten Principles for Success*, a philosophy that helps business people create balance and harmony within their workplaces and in their personal lives. She is the author of *The Forgotten Customer*, a definitive book on how to satisfy the internal as well as the external customer, and the How To series, step-by-step manuals on how to hire, develop and retain the top performers. Debra is a regularly featured HR columnist in three trade publications and in several franchise and association newsletters.

She is a member of the National Speaker's Association and has presented nearly 300 presentations and seminars to companies, franchises, associations and networking groups covering hiring, developing and retaining top performers, management issues and customer service. For her work in the graphics industry, Debra received the National Association of Quick Printers Industry Award of Distinction in 2003.

In 1995, Debra became the founding president of the Greater Tucson Chapter of the National Association of Women Business Owners. She is also affiliated with National Association of Professional Leadership, Society for Human Resource Management and the Printing Industries Association.

Debra was born in El Paso, Texas, but moved with her family to the Detroit area where she lived until 1994. She attended Central Michigan University.

As a partner with Debra Thompson in TG & Associates (and in marriage), Bill Greif brings an engineer's perspective to the business along with the experience of two prior successful careers. His first career in the U.S. Army included assignments in the states and overseas as a staff officer, project manager and unit commander. For three years he taught mathematics at the United States Military Academy at West Point. He retired in 1980 as a lieutenant colonel and started his second career, which included assignments as a functional manager and project manager in the aerospace industry. As a department manager he was responsible for leading the development of support processes and tools for all of the products of Raytheon Missile Systems Company in Tucson. Bill also served as leader of the Raytheon Engineering Training Guidance Team, establishing process training policy and managing course content for this 6,000 person engineering organization. He retired from Raytheon in 2002 to work full time in TG & Associates.

Bill's experiences in both careers provided him with a strong foundation in the principles of people management and leadership. Bill shares with Debra a strong belief that success in business is only achieved through the proper development, management and encouragement of the people in the business. Bill worked with Debra to develop *Thompson's Ten Principles for Success* and assisted in the editing of *The Forgotten Customer* and the How To series.

Bill has a Bachelor of Science in Mechanical Engineering from the University of Detroit and a Master of Science in Mechanical Engineering from Michigan State University. He is a graduate of the U.S. Army Command and General Staff College and the Department of Defense Systems Management College.

Debra Thompson and Bill Greif formed TG & Associates in 1995 because they recognized that small business owners were having increasing difficulty in complying with the demands for human resource services. It was patently clear that the easy days of finding, developing and retaining employees were over and that the discipline needed was not in the comfort zones of small business owners and managers.

At the outset, Debra and Bill evolved a process map for business success which became *Thompson's Ten Principles for Success*. While the Ten Principles clearly articulated all the steps that needed to be considered for business success, it became apparent that the real focus lay in three underlying elements:

- Every business needs a set of processes and procedures to cover how everything in the business is to be done.
- Every business needs the right set of employees developed to provide outstanding service to the internal customers.
- Every business needs frequent and healthy communication as the glue that holds it all together.

Debra and Bill began the development of services and products that would enable owners and managers to put those basic elements in place. They shaped their company, TG & Associates, to help business owners build exceptional customer loyalty from the inside out. In the company's formative years this objective drove the company planning and activities. Over time the company expanded its offerings to encompass other than small businesses by treating staff members and teams within larger companies as small businesses in their own right. The internal customer concept pervades all businesses, and the pursuit of internal customer satisfaction is central to business success.

Additionally, they worked to increase the understanding of business owners and managers in the importance of the people to their success. Seminars and articles on People Management—The Critical Skill were prepared to help business owners understand the themes and how to implement them in the workplace. Later, products were developed to help small business owners in specific industry segments achieve the same levels of human resource competence that larger companies can hire staffs to perform. Both Debra and Bill believe that focus on the people in the business is paramount to success and, without it, the best equipment and processes are doomed to failure. "Employer of choice" is the current buzzword that echoes the support of this belief in companies around the world.

As an adjunct to their other products and services, Debra and Bill have helped owners with the increasingly difficult process of hiring top performers. Their efforts resulted in the creation and validation of a model hiring process—a disciplined approach to hiring guaranteed to provide top employees. This hiring process includes the necessary tools to evaluate prospective candidates and defined benchmarks for optimum candidates. This process is the foundation for *No More Rotten Eggs: A Dozen Steps to Grade AA Talent Management.*

Now, TG & Associates proudly recognize that they have achieved their vision of becoming **The Experts in the Human Side of Business** among their clients. All of their efforts, products and services increase this awareness and help them help more people.

Debra and Bill reside in Tucson, Arizona, which has been their home since 1994.

RECIPES FOR SUCCESS SERIES—
WE MAKE HIRING EASIER!

Each supplemental hiring kit comes with the following tools specific to that position:

- Behavioral Based Interview Questions
- Complete Job Description
- "Classic" Job Profile
- Internet ad(s) for Recruiting
- Internet Prescreening Questions
- Telephone Prescreening Questions

Kits are being added, so check by regularly. If you don't see one that you're looking for, call us toll-free at 877.842.7762 and we'll help you out.

ORDER YOUR RECIPES FOR SUCCESS TODAY!

Purchase online at **www.tgassociates.com**

call toll-free **877.842.7762** or complete the

order form that follows and fax to **520.751.7515**

tg & associates
the human side of business

ORDER TODAY!

Fax order form: **520.751.7515** or Call Toll Free: **1.877.842.7762**

Order Online: www.tgassociates.com

ASSESSMENT & TESTING PRODUCTS		UNIT PRICE	QUANTITY	TOTAL
Full Personality Profile		$150.00		
Compatibility Profile		$100.00		
Additional Profiles (Executive Summary, Strengths & Limitations, How to Manage, Mgmt Quest., Sales Quest., General Quest., Mgmt Audit, Sales Audit, Tech Audit, CSR Audit, Call Center Audit, & Career Guide)		$50.00		
EQ-i Assessment		$200.00		
$ales Max Select & Develop Combo		$350.00		
$ales Max Select		$225.00		
$ales Max Development		$225.00		
PRODUCTS				
Publications	The Forgotten Customer E-Book	$14.95		
	How to Develop Top Performers	$29.95		
	How to Retain Top Performers	$29.95		
	HR Forms CD	$69.95		
	Individual HR Forms	$5.99 each		
Job Descriptions	Basic (9 Individual Job Descriptions)	$129.00		
	Deluxe (18 Individual Job Descriptions)	$199.00		
	Individual	$19.95		
Hiring Tool Kits	Recipes for Success Series: Customer Service Representative	$49.95		
	Recipes for Success Series: Production Manager	$49.95		
	Recipes for Success Series: Outside Sales Representative	$49.95		
	Recipes for Success Series: Digital Imaging Specialist	$49.95		
	Recipes for Success Series: General Manager	$49.95		
	Recipes for Success Series: Administrative Assistant	$49.95		
Employee Handbook		$1,500.00		
RECRUITING SERVICES				
Complete Recruiting Package		per Fee Schedule		
a la carte Recruiting Services		per Fee Schedule		
Background Checking		$150.00 each		

SUBTOTAL	
Tax (AZ residents add 8.1%)	
Shipping & Handling**	
TOTAL	

**Standard Shipping & Handling $10.00
Overnight Mail Extra

Name _____

Company (if applicable) _____

Billing Street Address _____

[BILLING ADDRESS MUST MATCH CREDIT CARD BILLING ADDRESS]

City _____ State _____ Zip / Postal Code _____

Area Code / Phone # _____ Area Code / Fax # _____

Email Address _____

FORM OF PAYMENT: ☐ MasterCard ☐ Visa ☐ American Express ☐ Discover

Account Number ☐☐☐☐ ☐☐☐☐ ☐☐☐☐ ☐☐☐☐   Exp Date ☐☐☐

Name as it appears on card _____

Signature _____